AF531793

Recalling the Forgotten

EDUCATION AND MORAL QUEST

Recalling the Forgotten
EDUCATION AND MORAL QUEST

Avijit Pathak

Recalling the Forgotten: Education and Moral Quest
Avijit Pathak

© Author

First Published 2009
Reprinted 2013
Reprinted 2019
Reprinted 2026

ISBN 978-81-89833-71-8 (Hb)

All rights reserved. No part of this book may be reproduced or transmitted, in any form or by any means, without prior permission of the publisher.

Published by
AAKAR BOOKS
28 E Pocket IV, Mayur Vihar Phase I
Delhi 110 091, India
www.aakarbooks.com

Printed at
D.K. Fine Art Press, Delhi

To my students who wish to
celebrate the vocation of teaching

Contents

Preface

Recalling the forgotten, one may allege, is like refusing to come to terms with what prevails; it is sheer nostalgia; it is conservative; it is reactionary. I, however, do not agree with this allegation. As a matter of fact, it all depends on what one recalls: conservative practices or radical dreams. As I see it, there are moments when we must recall the forgotten wisdom, renew it, enlighten ourselves, fight the present pathology, and move towards a better future. It is in this sense that in this book I have recalled the forgotten—the emancipatory ideals of education. It is by no means my contention to argue that these ideals were necessarily practised in some 'golden' era. Instead, I see these ideals more as possibilities and aspirations which seem to have been devalued and forgotten because of our present obsession with the market. Global capitalism and its culture of money-making/skill-oriented/instrumental learning have led to the commodification of education. Its consequences are devastating. It annihilates deeper aesthetic/ethical/spiritual ideals of learning; it negates criticality and reflexivity; it privileges instrumentality. No wonder, instead of elevating man to a spiritual height, it reduces him into a mere resource with an appropriate use-value. Recalling the forgotten emancipatory ideals of education is, therefore, not like regressing to a mythical past; instead, it is essentially an attempt to create a new future. It is a process—a deeply aesthetic/moral/spiritual quest.

A book of this kind, I am aware, would not appeal to those who have already decided that what prevails is necessarily true, valid and practical, and hence there is no need to alter it. Nor would it appeal to those who think that education is too much of a 'soft' domain, and hence without revolutionary changes in the 'hard' domain of political economy, an attempt to alter it is useless, or at best a utopian/idealistic venture. However, this book, I believe, is essentially for those—students, teachers, researchers, parents, policy-makers, educationists and social philosophers—who believe that 'base' and 'superstructure', far from being engaged in a purely causal/deterministic relationship, constitute an integrated whole, and education is, therefore, deeply significant for shaping our consciousness and priorities. Yes, the book makes it clear that it is desirable as well as possible to visualize an alternative, critique the dominance of the market through active pedagogic interventions, and restore the aesthetic/moral dimension of education. In other words, the book is for those who believe that revolution, far from being a spectacular event, is a continual process, and every day is a new beginning, and every effort—no matter how small—has its relevance. In fact, there is no ideal situation for initiating a change; we have to move even when obstacles are enormous.

The book has emerged out of a creative process in which I have been engaging for quite some time. My vocation—the vocation of teaching—requires perpetual reflection. What am I teaching? Why am I teaching what I am teaching ? Is it merely a cognitive/intellectual exercise? Is it just instrumental: a skill for earning a living? Or, is it far deeper—something that gives a higher purpose? All these questions make me reflect on the sociology/philosophy of education. True, I teach in a university. But then, the domain of school education, for me, is no less fascinating. It is this deep interest in school education that leads me to interact—and interact meaningfully—with school children, teachers and parents. I begin to take active interest in the entire process of the transaction of school knowledge: its texts, examinations, modes of evaluation, disciplinary practices, and classroom dynamics. Eventually, this interest gets transformed into a desire to intervene. With my students and friends I begin to conduct a series of workshops with school children. The entire exercise has given me immense insight into the inner world of children: their cognitive power, their emotional vulnerability, their hopes, anguish and excitement. In other words, I have collected what professional social science regards as primary data through this ongoing process: a deeply dialogic/humane/reflexive/qualitative engagement with education—its different sites, its academic practices, and its active participants. It is this dialogue that has given me the confidence to write this book.

Its style reflects its philosophy. It is dialogic; it transcends disciplinary boundaries; it unites social theory, philosophy and ethnography of everyday life. It is not statistical; it is qualitative, experiential and meditative. It is not impersonal; it is reflexive; it is a quest—a longing. 'Reason', wrote Allama Iqbal in one of his excellent poems, 'analyzes the secrets of life', whereas the 'heart sees these secrets before its own eyes.' Or, for that matter, reason 'explores the book of knowledge', and the heart 'pursues transcendental thought'. Possibly the book too makes an effort—a humble effort—to reconcile the two: reason and heart. And that is what my methodology is all about. To use the language of formal sociology, it has its roots in hermeneutic traditions, in critical realism, and in interpretative methods.

The book begins with an Introduction. It poses the moral questions confronting us, and situates the debate on education. In a way, it articulates the very purpose of the book. Chapter I is about an exploration into the social/philosophical discourses on education: its core ideals, the challenges that modernity brings about, the emerging pedagogic issues in the changing cultural landscape, and above all, the trajectory of educational discourses in Indian society. Chapter II pleads for a reflexive/critical pedagogy, examines the specificities of academic practices relating to science, mathematics, history, social science and literature, and finally explores the possibilities of an altogether different culture of schooling. Chapter III enters the domain of higher learning, throws light on the humanistic ideals of university education, examines the crisis of higher education in India, and then evolves alternatives to resist its growing marketization and commodification. And finally, in Conclusion an attempt has been made to see the radical potential of teaching as a vocation, and how it can arouse hope amidst despair. In other words, what unites all these chapters is a concern for the moral/aesthetic component of education which, I fear, has been overshadowed by the instrumentality of marketization.

As I have already indicated, a book of this kind is not possible without cultivating what I regard as the art of listening. I am indeed grateful to all those school students, parents and teachers who have given me the time to interact with them. With deep gratitude I recall the contributions made by my students—Deo Nath, Ravinandan, Gitika, Ram Babu, Bikram, Bimal and Suganya—who actively participated as resource persons in different workshops that we organized for school children. I always feel myself privileged because of my location in the Jawaharlal Nehru University. Yes, my colleagues across disciplines with whom I have shared my ideas are of great help; and the entire ambience of the university—its culture of debate and dialogue—has shaped my thinking. I also express my gratitude to Mr. Bharat Kumar for typing the manuscript. Mr. Saxena—the creative/enthusiastic leader of Aakar Books—has always fascinated me; his eagerness to publish meaningful social science texts is indeed remarkable. I am indeed happy that he has chosen to publish my book. And finally, my family members are of great moral support. My mother always enquires whether I am writing a new book; my sisters and brothers continue to expect something creative from me; and my nephews and nieces—particularly, Aairban, Keshav, Parul and Pallavi—have given their valuable insights. My wife's deep insights into the world of children, and her active participation in this project have given me the added strength. And Ananya—our daughter—has always narrated her school experiences, and participated in the ongoing discussion on education that keeps taking place almost every night at the time of dinner. This intense bond is my capital. If the book makes its presence felt, the credit must go to all of them.

Avijit Pathak

September 5, 2008 Jawaharlal Nehru University

New Delhi

Introduction

MORAL QUESTIONS : SITUATING THE DEBATE

There are primarily three ways through which I wish to reflect on moral/ethical questions which, I believe, are absolutely important for a deeper understanding of education: (a) the relationship between the individual and society; ((b) man's own inner struggle resulting from the dialectic of power and love, egotism and altruism, and desire and austerity; and (c) the mode of human engagement with nature.

When we think of the relationship between the individual and society, a series of moral/ethical questions begin to confront us: questions relating to human rights, democratic freedom, collective welfare, social justice and egalitarianism. Yes, in liberal/modern times we have been repeatedly warned of the dangers of the tyranny of collectivism: how in the name of the 'collective', be it a caste association or a religious group, one can be belittled, and deprived of one's creativity, uniqueness and freedom. Possibly a major aspiration of the age of modernity is the affirmation of the individual—her agency, her rights and her freedom. It is in this sense that modernity can indeed be said to be a liberating force rescuing the individual from the trap of excessive collectivism or communitarianism. It fights all sorts of religious orthodoxy and fatalism. It gives one the courage to question, and believe that life is a domain of possibilities. Indeed, modernity, for its enthusiastic proponents, is about freedom: freedom of the individual. But then, is the individual a discrete entity? Or, is one's freedom unbounded? It is in this context that I wish to refer to an illuminating sociological wisdom. 'Even though sociology as a formal/ academic discipline was a product of modern times, it did not forget to point out a more nuanced understanding of modernity—particularly the relationship between the individual and society. It did not deny the merits of individualism, or the doctrine of rights. But then, sociologists have repeatedly asserted that society is not and cannot be a mere collection or aggregate of individuals; society has its own sanctity and transcendent power that must locate individuals, and make them aware of the boundaries, or the historicity of their freedom. For example, we know how Emile Durkheim, despite his modern sensibilities relating to growing individuation, differentiation and division of labour in complex industrial societies, celebrated this 'social fact', and critiqued the principles of utilitarianism: the glorification of the atomized individual driven by the will to maximize his own pleasure (Durkheim 1933). 'If interest is the only ruling force', wrote Durkheim, 'each individual finds himself in a state of war with every other since nothing comes to mollify the egos, and any truce in this eternal antagonism would not be of long duration' (Ibid: 203-04). In fact, Durkheim made us aware of the limits to excessive individualism. It was like striving for an ethical balance that nurtures a meaningful engagement between the individual and society:

> Men cannot live together without acknowledging and consequently making mutual sacrifices, without tying themselves to one another with strong, durable bonds. Every society is a moral society... Because the individual is not sufficient unto himself, it is from society that he receives everything necessary to him, as it is for society that he works. Thus is formed a very strong sentiment of the state of dependence in which he finds himself. He becomes accustomed to estimating it as its just value, that is to say, in regarding himself as part of a whole, the organ of an organism. Such sentiments naturally inspire not only mundane scarifies which assure the regular development of daily social life, but, even on occasion, acts of complete self-renunciation and wholesale abnegation. On its side, society learns to regard its members no longer as things

> over which it has rights, but as co-operators whom it cannot neglect and towards him it owes duties (Ibid: 228).

Durkheim's moral sociology, we know, was not appreciated by all; conflict theorists saw the traces of 'conservatism' in his worldview; and phenomenologists were disturbed by the 'structuralist' element in his thinking. Yet, the fundamental issue he raised about the need for an ethical balance in the relationship between the individual and society could not be denied. Possibly the master thinker was making an attempt to recall what many modernists often forget: the need to see beyond the discourse of rights, and unite it with the ethos of collective concern or duties. If we emphasize only on duties, it is likely to promote submissiveness. Likewise, rights without duties can degenerate into a form of egotistic cult. In fact, the complex and dynamic relationship between the individual and society, rights and duties, or 'agency' and 'structure' remains a major sociological riddle to be solved (Giddens 1993). Even Karl Marx—a great modernist, and the darling of all radicals—could not give his consent to the doctrine of the self-centred individual insulated from the flow of collective existence. He critiqued 'alienation' and 'estrangement', saw beyond bourgeois individualism, and imagined communism as 'the genuine resolution of the conflict between man and man—the true resolution of the strife between existence and essence, between objectification and self-confirmation, between freedom and necessity, between the individual and species' (Marx 1977: 97). At a deeper existential level, it meant that the individual could affirm herself only in a life-affirming relationship with others, and society could become truly vibrant and alive by allowing individuals to evolve, grow and prosper. Neither naked individualism nor collectivist totalitarianism, but a culture of mutuality, reciprocity and relatedness was what Marx was striving for. In fact, to act ethically and morally is not just to think about oneself; it is also to think of others, and transcend the otherness of the other, and find a meaning of existence in a reciprocal bond between the self and the world. Look at Marx's prophetic message: 'If you love without evoking love in return—that is, if your loving as loving does not produce reciprocal love; if through a *living expression* of yourself as a loving person you do not make yourself a *beloved one*, then your love is impotent—a misfortune' (Ibid: 132). Yes, such an intense ethical/spiritual quest, I believe, has acquired urgency at a time when neo-liberalism, global capitalism and marketization have accelerated social Darwinism, and promoted the cult of egotistic self-interest, and narcissistic individualism.

Another important ethical question emanates from man's own inner struggle. Yes, the material/physical component of human personality, it can be argued, strives for power—instant gratification of desires and instincts. It knows nothing except itself. It is pleasure-seeking, restless and violent. But then, there is also a psychic/spiritual/aesthetic quest for something more subtle—peace, tranquility, merger and transcendence. It is this continual struggle that characterizes the human situation. For example, when we reflect on psychoanalysis—particularly Sigmund Freud's penetrating analysis of the human psyche—we come to know about this conflict which the celebrated thinker characterized as a conflict between *id* and *superego*, between *Thanatos* and *Eros*, between instincts and civilization (Freud: 1985). For Freud, man is essentially a conflict-ridden being, and the power of the *unconscious* filled with desires and impulses is irresistible, and the idea of a moral, peaceful, altruistic civilized being is more like a construct through which society represses man. To put it otherwise, the moral foundations of a civilization, as Freud would have argued, are bound to crumble through neurosis, phobia, anxiety, psychic disorder, violence and war:

> If more is demanded of a man, a revolt will be produced in him or a neurosis, or he will be made unhappy. The commandment, 'Love thy neighbour as thyself', is the strongest defence against human aggressiveness and an excellent example of the unpsychological proceedings of the cultural super-ego. The commandment is impossible to fulfil; such an enormous inflation of love can only lower its value, not get rid of the difficulty. Civilization pays no attention to all this; it merely admonishes us that the harder it is to obey the precept the more meritorious it is to do so. But anyone who follows

> such a precept in presentday civilization only puts himself at a disadvantage *vis-à-vis* the person who disregards it. What a potent obstacle to civilization aggressiveness must be, if the defence against it can cause as much unhappiness as aggressiveness itself! 'Natural' ethics, as it is called, has nothing to offer here except the narcissistic satisfaction of being able to think oneself better then others (Ibid: 337).

Yes, this debunking of moral principles was like a shock, something that we also experienced when Friedrich Nietzsche, much before Freud, came with his notion of *superman* driven by the 'will to power'—the superman who loathes 'the petty virtues' and 'the petty prudences', and instead, asserts that 'life itself is *essentially* appropriation, injury, overpowering of the strange and weaker, suppression, severity, imposition of one's own forms, incorporation and, at the least and mildest, exploitation' (Nietzsche 1981: 229-30).

But then, as I wish to argue, this is only one narrative about human vulnerability, about the supremacy of aggression over peace, power over reciprocity, and narcissism over relatedness. It should not be forgotten that there is yet another narrative which, unlike that of a Freud or a Nietzsche, tells a different story: a story of possibilities, a story of human evolution from darkness to light, from egotism to altruism, from violence to peace and tranquility.[1] In a way, it is also a central concern of mystics, spiritualists and even profound humanists. It would be argued that man is capable of overcoming the limitedness of his own little world, and experiencing something higher, nobler and wider. In our own Indian philosophy, to take a striking example, we often speak of the three *gunas* born of *prakrti*—*tamas, rajas* and *sattva*—that bind down in the body (*Bhagavadgita. XIV*). *Tamas* is about inertia and darkness leading to 'unillumination, inactivity, negligence and mere delusion' (Ibid: 13); *rajas* is about passion and vitality which result in 'greed, unrest and cravings' (Ibid: 12); and *sattva* is about calmness and peace. And life's journey ought to be a movement towards *sattva* through a series of moral/ethical practices. Not solely that. A liberated soul transcends even *sattva* because he is beyond all *gunas*. Until we reach this stage, as it is believed, we are only in the making; our evolution is incomplete. It is an ideal that is heavily demanding—an urge to become like a yogi 'who regards pain and pleasure alike, who dwells in his own self, who looks upon a clod, a stone, a piece gold as of equal worth, who remains the same amidst the pleasant and the unpleasant things, who is of firm mind, who regards both blame and praise as one' (Ibid: 24).

It is this quest that is seen in all grand ideals of love, devotion and prayer. How to see beyond one's little self, and embrace others is a moral quest. Or, how to pass through the conflict between darkness and light, and move towards a higher state of being is a question that continues to have its impact on our moral sensibilities. What a wonderful interpretation of this conflict Mohandas Karamchand Gandhi made when he reflected on the *Bhagavadgita*:

> Personally, I believe that Duryodhana and his supporters stand for the Satanic impulses in us, and Arjuna and others stand for Goddward impulses. The battlefield is our body. The poet-seer, who knows from experience the problems of life, has given a faithful account of the conflict which is eternally going on within us. Shri Krishna is the Lord dwelling in everyone's heart who is ever murmuring. His promptings in a pure *chitta* look like a clock ṭicking in a room. If the clock of the *chitta* is not wound up with the key of self-purification, the in-dwelling lord no doubt remains where He is, but the ticking is heard no more (Gandhi 1982: 13-14).

And this quest, I would argue, has acquired added relevance in our times, particularly because we see the all-pervasive commodification and consumerism that generates violence and restlessness through constant simulation, stimulates the aggressive urge to fulfil one's egotistic desires, and makes one believe that 'life has no goal except the one to move, no principle except the one of fair exchange, no satisfaction except the one to consume' (Fromm 1985:89).

The mode of human engagement with nature is yet another domain that leads to moral and ethical questions. It is true that we live in the age of science and modernity, and it asserts man's scientific rationality, technological intelligence and supremacy over nature. Yes, in a way, modulating, shaping, dominating and conquering nature has become an integral component of the 'civilizing' process. And it has led to immense techno-industrial development and heightened standard of living. It is also true that this techno-scientific skill has helped humankind to survive, and overcome the forces of nature which, at times, are damaging to human safety, security and growth. If we recall our utter helplessness before the wild forces of nature in pre-modern times, it is said, we would invariably remain grateful to what science and technology have done to enrich human life! Yet, it should not be forgotten, there is a dialectic in the entire process. The same liberating forces—if exercised excessively, and without a sense of humility—can prove to be utterly destructive. It is like despiritualizing nature, and reducing it into a mere 'resource' for man's continual material well-being. Nature, Francis Bacon argued with immense zeal, must be 'bound into service' and made a slave, put 'in constraint', and 'moulded' by the mechanical arts. Or, for that matter, as Rene Descartes thought, there is no fundamental difference 'between the machines made by craftsmen and the various bodies that nature alone composes'. No other relationship—say a creative/delicate relationship—with nature is possible anymore. It has to be perpetually utilized; its resources have to be exhausted, and this victory must go on indefinitely. No wonder, the principle of aggression is implicit in the dominant notion of development. It conquers everything: trees and forests, rivers and mountains, plants and animals. It annihilates memories and mythologies. Its only motto is limitless 'growth' which dispassionate economists quantify; and this magical number is enough for governments to carry on their developmental projects—building huge dams, occupying fertile lands for constructing Special Economic Zones, demolishing old habitats for decorating the urban space. Is it, therefore, surprising that today a series of moral/ethical issues have begun to emerge: issues relating to development, environmental disaster, standard of living, displacement, rehabilitation, and above all, ways of relating to nature? In fact, the anguish over the demystification of nature can be felt in the language of what we often regard as the other West—the language of romanticism relating to the enchantment of nature and a living relationship with it, an intense poetic imagination that once led Walt Whitman to write:

To me every hour of the light and dark is a miracle.
Every cubic inch of space is a miracle.
Every square yard of the surface of the earth is spread with the same.
Every foot of the interior swarms with the same,
To me the sea is a continual miracle.
The fishes that swim—the rocks—the motion of the waves—
The ships with men in them,
What stranger miracles are there? (Whitman 1986:389)

As a matter of fact, it was also the language of philosophic anarchists and utopians like Emmersen and Thoreau. And yes, contemporary neo-leftists, ecofeminists and environmentalists have repeatedly warned us of the dangers of 'instrumental' orientation to nature, and celebrated the ethos of balance, harmony and understanding. Again, when we look at some of the ancient texts—say, the Vedic hymns relating to the adoration of nature, we witness a similar spirit of reverence, wonder and respect.[2] These voices, let it be clear, are not recalled here to relinquish science, and celebrate an idealized living in the lap of nature. The fact is that the questions which are emerging are critical and deeper. Can we keep looking at nature in the same way as we have been doing, particularly for the last four hundred years? Can we go on destroying the ecological balance —the entire natural landscape and its biodiversity in the name of 'development'? These are complex questions having moral, economic and political implications. But then, these questions can no longer be escaped. Possibly this requires a high degree of moral/ethical sensibility: an attitude of self-restraint and balance, an alternative principle of economics and standard of living, a spirit of living engagement with nature, or what a contemporary social scientist has regarded as 'core ecological values' implying: (i) living in harmony with nature, (ii) overcoming anthropocentric prejudice, and (iii) recognizing intrinsic value in beings other than humans (Hayward 1994 : 31-32).

These three ethical principles—a reciprocal relationship between the individual and society, an inner quest for peace and harmony, and a creative engagement with nature—are not isolated and separated. In fact, all these three principles constitute a whole, and indicate what can be regarded as a spirit of merger—seeing beyond one's little self, and experiencing an intimate bond with the larger reality which manifests itself in the dynamics of human relationship, or in the vastness of natural milieu. It is like striving for a culture that values solidarity, egalitarianism, ecological balance and human fulfilment in love and tranquility. 'Why is it that all good things—Gandhism, Marxism, socialism, environmentalism and spiritualism—collapse? And why is it that we continue to cherish the glamour of capitalism: its market, its technology, its comfort, its aggression? Or, why is it that in the struggle between the good and the evil, it is always the evil that wins?' As a young learner—a school student of Class XII—asks me this pertinent question, I find no immediate answer. I, however, begin to realize the importance of a quest for alternative values which, I guess, can make the young learner and her generation think, feel, act and dream differently.

And my central argument in this book is that education has to play a key role in this transformative process. I insist on this point because in the name of 'determining' causes like techno-economic and other material factors, there is a tendency to undermine the significance of education in the process of social transformation. For instance, it is believed—particularly by techno-economists and even by a section of orthodox Marxists—that our beliefs, attitudes and worldviews are primarily dependent on the economy and technology, and hence no significant result is likely to come if we work in the 'soft' domain of education without looking at the 'hard' reality. I do not wish to enter into the age-old philosophic debate between the materialists and idealists. What I am pleading for is rather simple and straight. It is for a more dialogic and dialectical interplay of economy and culture. It is not a question of either/or. Instead, it is a realization that for any project of social transformation we need to work with equal intensity in the domain of education: the way we think, define ourselves and relate to the world. In fact, among the Marxists it was Antonio Gramsci who realized and spoke of this truth rather convincingly because he knew the importance of cultural hegemony, and the resultant need to work in the domain of culture to transform human society (Gramsci 1971). In fact, Gramsci saw 'primitive infantilism' in economic determinism. The domain of culture, as this creative Marxist asserted, is an important terrain on which men move, acquire consciousness of their position, and struggle. And particularly in our times when civil society and cultural/educational institutions have become immensely powerful, as Gramsci would have reminded us, there is an urgent need for the 'war of position': a struggle in the domain of ideas and consciousness. No wonder, for him, education was absolutely important in diffusing a socialist 'counter-hegemony' among all potentially revolutionary subjects. Gramsci was just an example from the Marxian tradition. As a matter of fact, if we look at the history of ideas, we do realize how the possibilities implicit in the domain of education fascinated a series of thinkers and activists—from Leo Tolstoy to Mohandas Karamchand Gandhi, from Ivan Illich to Paulo Freire. We were repeatedly reminded of the transformative power of education.

My book begins with this possibility or with this hope: much can be done in the domain of education. At a deeper level, education, as I would argue, is essentially about the moral/ethical quest: a process of transforming our consciousness, our beliefs, aspirations and orientations to the world. True, none would dispute that such liberating education is a life-long process, and we continue to learn through diverse experiences in politics, family, sexuality and spirituality. Love and separation, disease and recovery, and struggle and resistance: every major episode in life is a turning point, and gives us illuminating lessons. In this informal/experiential mode—passing through the complex trajectory of life, seeing a film, listening to a piece of music, and reading a novel—we learn great moral lessons. It is in this sense that education has a much broader connotation than its merely formal/academic component. But then, I would argue that even formal education—the way a complex society expects us to pass through well-defined stages of school/university learning—cannot escape the moral/ethical question. It is wrong to think that formal education is only about academic/technical skills, and there is necessarily a separation between academic methods and ethical pursuits. Because all these skills which we value today—say, the skill of a doctor, an engineer, a scientist, a manager or a historian—have to be operationalized and practised in a concrete socio-historical setting, and if we do not reflect on life's deeper objectives, these skills may prove to be useless, or even utterly disastrous. For example, how often we have seen a 'skilled' scientist allowing himself to be hijacked by the military establishment to further accelerate the growth of technologies of mass destruction; a management graduate joining the lucrative corporate world only to sell soaps and wine; or a doctor with his specialized skills taking active part in the unholy act of female infanticide! In other words, it is like living in a strange world in which the continual production of 'specialists' and 'experts' does not necessarily assure human connectedness, creativity and love.

As a matter of fact, in the ultimate analysis, it is our creative and critical orientation, or our moral sensibilities that would shape how we use these 'skills', and enrich our world. That is why, divorcing formal education from deeper moral and philosophical queries would be utterly damaging. This does not mean that morality demands religious education. Nor does it mean that ethical sensibilities have to be cultivated through sermonizing. Anyone engaged with education knows how authoritarian and life-negating such moral learning can prove to be. Life has to be lived, felt and experienced, and not reduced into a series of moral axioms to be bombarded on the mind of the young learner by an authoritarian teacher. In fact, for ethical questions, what we need is just a sensitive/dialogic process of learning when we study science and economics, engage in mathematics, or look at history. As I would argue in this book, all these branches of knowledge—from mathematics to literature, from history to physics—which we include as part of 'legitimate' curriculum in formal educational institutions have their deeper philosophic and ethical meanings. And with a radical pedagogy, these academic disciplines can indeed act like a catalyst, and arouse our moral sensibilities

NOTES

1. Even though Sigmund Freud was an outstanding thinker, his ideas need not be regarded as universal. He was a product of his times. In fact, his reactive and negative attitude towards accepted cultural values, it is argued, was due to the historical conditions which immediately preceded him. For example, his conception of man as conflict-ridden and potentially neurotic, it seems, was a reaction against the Victorian tendency to see everything in a rosy light and yet to describe everything *sub rosa*. As Carl Jung put it, 'if Freud is viewed in this retrospective way as an exponent of the new century against the old, with its illusions, its hypocrisy, its half-truths, its faked, overwrought emotion, its sickly morality, its bogus, sapless religiosity, and its lamentable taste, he can be seen, in my opinion, much more correctly than when one marks him out as the herald of new ways and new truths' (Jung 1967 : 35-36). No wonder, psychoanalysis has moved beyond Freud. And its creative engagement with spiritual traditions and even Marxism has led to a more positive notion of man filled with human possibilities. Jung, Fromm, Marcuse and Maslow, it would not be wrong to say, did reveal this possibility.
2. Nature, let us not forget, nurtures and sustains us. Nature arouses poetry and imagination—a sense of humility and an urge to pray. I often recall the Vedic hymns, and experience the beauty of this enchantment. Look at these hymns:

   Upward, O Agni, rise thy flames, pure and resplendent,
   blazing high.
   Thy lustres, fair effulgences (RV. VIII: 44.17).

   Or

   Bless us with shine, bless us with perfect day light, bless us
   with cold, with fervent heat and lustre.
   Bestow on us, O Surya, varied riches, to bestow us in
   our home and when we travel (RV.X:37.10)

Chapter I

Rediscovering Educational Goals: A Quest for Fundamental Ideals

What does it mean to be 'educated'? Well, it is always possible to argue that education is a process of transmission and communication of social heritage from one generation to another; education—particularly, formal education—is an important means of socialization in a complex society that extends beyond family-kinship networks, and demands our adherence to abstract/universal principles; and education is also about entering the ever-expanding frontiers of knowledge in diverse fields. But then, a 'pragmatic' answer that often emerges, and tends to occupy our consciousness is that an 'educated' person is essentially one who acquires a skill, gets a degree from a formal site of learning, and thereby earns one's livelihood. In other words, education, as it is argued, means enhanced capital leading to improved social status, occupational mobility and material success. This popular imagination manifests itself when schools advertise their 'success' stories, marketize their 'products', and courses are being evaluated in terms of their saleability.[1] Even though this instrumental thinking reigns supreme in our times, not everyone agrees with this trend; there is a deep-rooted feeling shared by many educationists, philosophers and revolutionaries that education ought to have a much broader ideal to follow. It is not just about skill-learning and money-making; it is also about inner light, about wisdom, and about profound sensitivity. To put it otherwise, from the mere externality of education—degree, job, money—the focus is shifted to deeper experiences: how one thinks, feels, dreams, acts and intervenes. The ethico-moral dimension of education, therefore, gains immense significance. And this chapter too acquires its relevance precisely because it seeks to see beyond the instrumentality of the existing trend, and reminds us of the deeper ideals of education which, I believe, have to be asserted with immense zeal in order to create a just society.

I
CORE IDEALS

To begin with, let us identify a set of core ideals which have been repeatedly emphasized (of course, with varying degree of emphasis) by all great proponents of emancipatory education. As a matter of fact, a journey to the philosophy of education would enable us to abstract a set of four core principles—*critical consciousness*, *aesthetic imagination*, *inner awakening* and *sensitivity to vocation*—from its extraordinarily rich discourses which have been evolving through diverse traditions and visionary thoughts. It is in this context that we need to remember that a great ideal of education is that it expands the capacity of human thinking. We no longer remain contented with the way things appear to us. We seek to understand, interpret and explain the world. We penetrate, go deeper, and ask questions. In other words, education is about the cultivation of critical spirit: perpetual eagerness, curiosity and restlessness to explore. In modern times we often equate this spirit with scientific temper. Because science, its proponents argue, evolves as it does not take the world for granted. It questions, explains, demystifies ...It does not remain contented in the name of discovering the absolute truth. Instead, as Karl Popper argued with a great degree of sophistication, science progresses because of its inherent principle of refutability; it perpetually strives for new findings to replace a set of conjectures with a new one (Popper 1972). It is this criticality which has played an important role in liberating our consciousness from dogmas and superstitions.

At this juncture, however, I wish to make a point of caution. The ideal of criticality as liberating consciousness can be equated with scientific temper, provided we broaden the meaning of science, and do not equate it solely with the technological mastery over nature which, at times, becomes devoid of reflexivity and criticality. As a matter of fact, the kind of critical spirit we are taking about can be seen in people working in diverse domains of life: not just natural scientists and technologists, but poets, saints, revolutionaries and other creative souls. It is in this context that I wish to recall Nachiketa's intense zeal: his urge to understand the meaning of death, and his refusal to get carried away by any delusion, or temptation like 'cattle in plenty, elephants, gold and horses' or 'noble maidens with charity and musical instruments' (KU.I:1.23-1.25). And we know from the extraordinary tale of the *Katha Upanishad* that it was this curiosity and single-minded devotion that eventually convinced Yama to explain the great secret to him. Nachiketa gave us a great ideal of learning which has its appeal because, to use the language of contemporary educationists, developing the capacity for critical thinking is important for separating the trivial from the serious, the meaningful from the substantial. Nachiketa did not take things far granted. Nor did he remain contented with 'normal' things of life. Instead, with absolute sincerity he was questioning and questioning in order to separate the trivial from the substantial. Even though not a 'scientist' in contemporary sense of the term, his curiosity/ eagerness was an ideal no educationist could remain indifferent to. It is true that this questioning mind—the refusal to remain contented with the surface reality—does not necessarily have a smooth and comfortable trajectory. Because not to agree with the given order of things is to suffer, and experience even ridicule and marginalization. We know Nachiketa suffered; so did Socrates and Galileo and many others who questioned, interrogated and made us think. Yet, I would argue that the inherent experience of pain and suffering notwithstanding, the ideal of critical spirit gives us the courage to fight, and move ahead in life. That is why, criticality is not cynicism; nor is it merely what contemporary postmodernists regard as 'deconstruction'. It is essentially about seeing a new possibility, and constructing a new world. It is filled with unbounded optimism that we see, to take just two striking illustrations, in Gandhi's creative 'experiments' with life, and in Marx's penetrating dialectical mind that passes through conflicts and contradictions, and yet evolves a path towards a just society.[2] Education is about having hope in human possibilities—not shallow hope, but hope emanating from critical consciousness.

It is also important to realize that together with critical consciousness, education ought to arouse aesthetic imagination: a sense of beauty and wonder. Because to live meaningfully is to experience the rhythm of life, and to engage with it creatively. This is what makes human life qualitatively different from mere survival. As Marx wrote in his characteristic style, 'Animals produce under the dominion of immediate physical need, whilst man produces even when he is free from physical need and only truly produces in freedom therefrom' (Marx 1977:74). Or, as Marx added, 'man produces objects in accordance with the laws of beauty' (Ibid: 74). It is this aesthetic urge that has created some of the finest forms of art, music and literature. But when I am speaking of aesthetic imagination, I do not wish to limit myself merely to its celebrated manifestations in poetry, painting, sculpture and other art forms. I wish to see it in everyday life itself: the way a gardener works with plants and flowers, a mother nurtures her child, or a farmer cultivates his land. Because, as a great art teacher once reminded us, 'Every act done with a sense of beauty, grace and human relevance is art, and every object created with care is an artefact' (Devi Prasad 1998: 7). As a matter of fact, aesthetic imagination is one's capacity to transform what otherwise appears to be mundane and routinized into something beautiful and meaningful. Without this aesthetic sensibility life becomes boring; there is no new moment; each day becomes like any other day devoid of beauty, imagination and wonder, and then, as existentialists would have argued, the spectre of 'absurdity' begins to haunt man. To have aesthetic education is, therefore, to restore meaning in life, to evolve a way of seeing, feeling and relating to the world. Devi Prasad gave a beautiful example to make this point abundantly clear before us:

> I had a friend during my student days who was born blind. Occasionally, I used to go for a walk with him in the evenings. Often he would suddenly stop under a tree and ask, "Brother, is there something here?" Or he would ask, "Are we standing

> under a tree?" Or "Is there a house on our right?" This young man could not see, he did not even know what a tree or a house looked like to those with eyesight, however defective. He never had any visual experience. But he was aware of the existence of things around. It is this kind of awareness that helps us to be sensitive about things outside ourselves (Ibid: 16).

Indeed, this 'awareness' or realization of 'grace in life' makes our existence aesthetically significant and meaningful. It is, therefore, not surprising that many creative minds all over the world did speak of aesthetic education. Rabindranath Tagore, I believe, was a great champion of this ideal. His celebration of nature—its abundance and its beauty—was remarkable. He disliked the monotony of artificial learning: a school- mediated culture in which children are caged. Instead, his great thirst for colour, for music, for movement of life inspired him to develop in the children 'the freshness of their feeling of Nature, a sensitiveness of soul in their relationship with their human surroundings, with the help of literature, festive ceremonials and also the religious teaching which enjoins us to come to the nearer presence of the world through the soul, thus to gain it more than can be measured—like gaining an instrument, not merely by having it, but by producing music upon it' (Tagore 1983b: 26). Indeed, this is a great ideal of education. A sense of beauty and creativity softens the mind, arouses a feeling of calmness and harmony, and enables us to see beyond the utilitarian logic of hard calculation. It is in this sense that the light of aesthetic education makes us truly humane: full of love and ecstasy. Because, as the poet felt, 'everywhere in this earth the spirit of Paradise is awake and sending forth its voice', and it has to be seen 'in the sunlight and the green of the earth, in the beauty of the human face and the wealth of human life, even in objects that are seemingly insignificant and unprepossessing' (Tagore 1983a: 17).

Another great ideal of education is its ability to provide inner strength: the capacity to look at the inner world, understand the dynamics of one's inner being, and cope with the riddles of human existence: life and death, love and suffering, and unity and separation. It is about realizing one's location in the cosmos, and the urge to evolve a meaning of existence that transcends all that is temporal and fleeting. At times, it is being regarded as the spiritual component of education. Even when in a secular/scientific age we speak of externally visible and tangible markers of education (acquisition of professional skills, measured/quantified intelligence and aptitude, and certificates conveying different stages of graded learning one has passed through) there is a deep-rooted feeling that education remains incomplete without wisdom, and it should make us sufficiently mature to understand the deeper meaning of existence, and distinguish truth from falsehood, and eternal from temporal. Without an awareness of this profound meaning of existence, life loses its significance. No wonder, for a sociologist like Max Weber, it was 'disenchantment'; or for existentialist philosophers, it was 'absurd'; or, as we are experiencing in our times, in the magic world of global capitalism it is man's utter void manifesting itself in 'conspicuous consumption'!

As a matter of fact, without this ideal—no matter how demanding and spiritual it may sound—the notion of education remains superficial and fragmented: merely an outer appearance, but not truly substantial. In Indian philosophic thought we have witnessed this emphasis: the distinction between *vidya* and *avidya*, truth and *maya*, eternity and temporality, and inner realization and mere intellectual perception. When Truth—the knowledge of the Self or the Eternal and the Absolute—is felt and realized, it is believed, everything else is known; one acquires immense strength to cope with death, suffering and tragedy; one remains stable, no longer disturbed by all that is temporal and fleeting; one realizes the limitedness of one's finite ego, overcomes all sorts of duality and separation, and experiences a merger with the infinite. Yajnavalkya expressed this ideal in a remarkably brilliant fashion:

> For where there is duality as it were, there one smells another, there one sees another, there one hears another, there one thinks of another, there one understands another. Where, verily, everything has become the Self, then by what and whom should one smell, then by what and whom should one see, then by

> what and whom should one hear, then by what and to whom should one speak, then by what and on whom should one think, then by what and whom should one understand? By what should one know that by which all is known? By what, my dear, should one know the knower (BU. II: 4.14)?

It is this ideal of education that recurs in the *Upanishads*, in the epics, in the *Puranas*, and even in folklores. Even when it is excessively demanding, it gives dignity to the ideal of education. Because it asserts that education is not just about socialization, or about acquiring a skill; it is also about an inner quest. Without wisdom, what is the purpose of education? I often recall yet another Upanishadic story of Svetaketu Aruneya. He became a pupil at the age of twelve, and for the next twelve years studied all the Vedas. He, however, became arrogant, and began to think himself well-read. And then one day, the great sage Uddalaka who was his father asked him: 'Svetaketu, since you are now so greatly conceited, think yourself well-read and arrogant, tell me by which the unhearable becomes heard, the unpredictable becomes perceived, the unknowable becomes known' (CU.VI: 1.1-1.3). Svetaketu's snobbery began to collapse; yes, he knew words, but never did he internalize and realize their deeper significance. He had no answer to his father's query. It was at this crucial juncture that his real quest began to develop. And eventually, because of his father's role as a catalyst, he could realize what ought to be known: 'by one clod of clay all that is made of clay becomes known or by one nugget of gold, all that is made of gold becomes known, the modification being only a name arising from speech, while the truth is that it is just clay or gold' (CU. VII: 1.4-1.5). Svetaketu internalized the ultimate Truth transcending all differences and limitedness.

Yes, this narrative does remind us of the necessity of a journey towards a subtle state of being: eternally calm, peaceful and contented. And even if we do not feel comfortable with its 'mystical' or 'spiritual' elements, its essence—how to overcome perpetual fluctuations of the human mind and resultant violence, and realize a profound unity with the larger reality, or how to relate the finite to the infinite, or the temporal to the eternal—continues to have its appeal to many educationists, even though, unlike the Upanishadic sages, they may be speaking in purely modern/secular idioms.

However, life, we all know, cannot be merely contemplative. It is about the unity of theory and practice, contemplation and action, and spiritual and material. That is why, another important ideal of education is to prepare one for a meaningful and effective engagement with the phenomenal world with its diverse domains of activity. It is in this sense that there is a distinctively vocational dimension of education. A vocation, let it be realized, is not merely a job or an occupation; it has a deeper significance. I would think that it means primarily three things: (a) an inner calling, or an awareness of what can be regarded as one's *swadharma*;(b) a sense of creative accomplishment in what one does; and (c) willingness to contribute to human welfare through one's active and enthusiastic work. Take an example to understand the depth of a vocation. When we say that one is merely employed as a doctor, and when we say that one has found one's vocation in being a doctor, we indicate two different experiences. The fact that one is merely employed as a doctor is not essentially different from the fact that one could have been employed as an engineer or an administrator, or for that matter, anything else. One is only doing a job, and one is doing it because, say, it is prestigious or lucrative. One is not so much bothered about one's creativity, or about one's *swadharma*. An experience of this kind does not have much thrill and intensity: it is generally routinized, and more often then not, alienated. In contrast, when one feels that being a doctor is like realizing one's inner self, it touches one's mind, one's body, one's entire being; it inspires one to give one's best to the world. One feels that one has finally found one's vocation; it is not just an occupation; it is far deeper; it is a state of being that brings a sense of creative accomplishment. To quote John Dewey:

> To find out what one is fitted to do and to secure an opportunity to do it is the key to happiness. Nothing is more tragic than failure to discover one's true business in life, or to find that one has drifted or been forced by circumstances into an uncongenial calling. A right occupation means simply that the aptitudes of a person are in adequate play, working with the

minimum of friction and the maximum of satisfaction. With reference to other members of a community, this adequacy of action signifies, of course, that they are getting the best service the person can render (Dewey 1966:308).

It is, of course, true that finding one's vocation is no easy proposition. It does not happen one fine morning. Life is not necessarily a linear path; it has its turning points and puzzling curves. As Dewey would have argued, finding one's vocation 'will be a constant process as long as growth continues' (Ibid: 311). But then, educators can always act like a catalyst, and inspire the learner to realize that life is essentially this quest; it is an endeavour to hear one's inner all, and find one's vocation. It is to respect the uniqueness, specificity and importance of diverse vocations, and not to fit everybody in the same box. It is to give moral/emotional/intellectual support to the learner so that she can experiment with diverse possibilities, and eventually succeed in choosing what she is inclined to. This ideal of education has acquired special importance at a time when purely utilitarian considerations like money, glamour and saleability are causing homogeneity in ambitions, and preventing young learners from acquiring the courage to differ and experiment[3].

All these four core ideals constitute an integrated whole, and take us nearer to an understanding of what I wish to regard as ethically sensitive, socially productive, critical education. For instance, without aesthetic imagination, scientific education may prove to be utterly instrumental and violent towards nature. Again, without a journey to the inner world, education tends to become a mere technique of mastery over the outer world. Yet, at the same time, in the absence of critical consciousness, the inner quest for harmony may get reduced into an escape route from the real contradictions of the world. Likewise, without practical engagement through vocations, there is no point of merger between theory and practice, contemplation and action, art and technology, the transcendental and the empirical. In this sense all these four ideals are needed to reinforce one another.

These core ideals are the fundamentals from where I wish to begin. But then, society keeps moving, historically specific challenges emerge, and new moral dilemmas confront us. That is why, these ideals have to be activated and creatively modulated to cope with the changing time. In other words, through a creative interplay of sociology and philosophy, I would now examine the pedagogic implications of the dynamic socio-historical context in which a morally sensitive educator finds herself.

II
MODERNITY AND NEW CHALLENGES

To begin with, let us make sense of modernity—the way it poses specific challenges to educators. Modernity, social scientists often argue, does not necessarily have a singular/standardized form; there are multiple modernities, and the way a society modernizes itself depends on its historicity, its cultural particularities. Yet, despite these diverse forms, there are certain core values and aspirations common to all modern societies (Pathak 2006). For example, no society, if it seeks to modernize itself, can defend itself without celebrating the 'rights' of the individual. An individual ought to have her own space: her unique/specialized needs, aptitudes, preferences and capabilities. Not surprisingly, modern societies all over the world have generated a high degree of differentiation, specialization and complex form of division of labour. From ascription to achievement, from passivity to reflexivity, from a mere receiver to an active initiator, from a victim of stereotypes to a creative being capable of making choices—this historic journey distinguishes modernity, and no society can negate its liberating potential. Yet, as I have said earlier, no individual, irrespective of the assertion of 'agency', can exist without the thread of connectedness that society creates. Despite our individuality and specialization, we need to live together, and share some binding norms and values. That is why, the challenge is to restore a shared culture which, at the same time, respects the autonomy of the individual. How do we consolidate the moral foundation of a society that is otherwise modern, secular and extraordinarily complex?

In this context I wish to refer to Emile Durkheim once again because he was remarkably sensitive to this question. In fact, a central theme in all his major sociological works was precisely this moral quest. Durkheim knew that 'mechanical solidarity' could not work in a modern society. At the same time, a modern society could not run on the basis of selfishness or the utilitarian notion of the self-centred atomized individual which could only lead to what he would have regarded as normlessness or 'anomic' disorder. For him, the real answer was 'organic solidarity' that, far from negating differences, would emerge out of the very need for interdependence in an otherwise specialized cultural milieu:

> It is quite otherwise with the solidarity which the division of labour produces. Whereas the previous type (mechanical solidarity) implies that individuals resemble each other, this type (organic solidarity) presumes their difference. The first is possible only in so far as the individual personality is absorbed into the collective personality, the second is possible only if each has a sphere of action which is peculiar to him: that is, a personality. It is necessary, then, that the collective conscience leaves open a part of the individual conscience in order that special functions may be established there, functions which it cannot regulate. The more this region is extended, the stronger is the cohesion which results from this solidarity. In effect, on the one hand, each one depends as much more strictly on society as labour is more divided; and, on the other, the activity of each is as much more personal as it is more specialized (Durkheim 1933: 131).

As a matter of fact, Durkheim was striving for a thread of connectedness, a shared culture amidst differences because, as he believed with absolute conviction, 'the duties of the individual towards himself are, in reality, duties towards society' (Ibid: 399). It was like asserting that 'the ideal of human fraternity can be realized only in proportion to the progress of the divison of labour' (Ibid: 406). It was in this context that Durkheim gave a new meaning to the debate on education. Yes, education must fulfil our modern needs and aspirations, and train us for diverse and specialized occupations. But then, education, as he asserted, was more than this specialized training; it must sensitize us, arouse a sense of collectivity amongst us, and inculcate the shared aspirations and values of the larger society. The object of education, he wrote in no uncertain terms, 'is to arouse and to develop in the child a certain number of physical, intellectual and moral states which are demanded of him by both the political society as a whole and the special milieu for which he is specifically destined' (Durkheim 1956:71). Education ought to serve an ethical function; it must consolidate the moral foundation of society; or to use his own words, 'to the egoistic and asocial being that has just been born it must, as rapidly as possible, add another, capable of leading a moral and social life' (Ibid: 72). Not surprisingly then, Durkheim wrote extensively on moral education, on school as a site of socialization in a modern society; the dynamics of the classroom, the social significance of the teaching community, and the entire ethos of discipline and punishment (Durkheim 1961). Education, he repeatedly asserted, should transform us, make us see beyond our little interests, and enable us to internalize the moral authority of the collective which, for him, transcends the individual.

The moral question that Durkheim posed, I believe, is immensely revealing. Because the age of modernity we live in poses precisely this question: how do we live together when there is heightened sense of individuation, specialization and occupational differentiation? Is education merely a training for specialized occupations? Durkheim raised these questions without any ambiguity, and made us sensitive to the challenge of education in modern times. Well, there is a point when his critics notice some sort of moral conservatism in his sociological agenda. Yet, what we cannot overlook is that more than anyone else, it was Emile Durkheim who gave us moral sensitivity to see the broader social function of education, and explore the possibility of a shared realm of togetherness. Yes, our children must strive for their specific careers. However, life is not just about becoming a doctor or a fashion designer or an engineer; life is also about experiencing, feeling and internalizing our shared memories, histories and struggles. Should we negate this societal component of education, and become only smart professionals? Possibly Durkheim would have wanted us to strive for a world in which a doctor recites Tagore before a patient, a fashion designer initiates a debate on Gandhi's clothes, and an engineer publishes poems in literary magazines. This fusion of horizons rescues us from discrete specialized roles, and enables us to consolidate the moral foundation of our society. With Durkheim we could indeed interrogate the merely instrumental/technical definition of education as just an occupational training.

At this juncture, we should not forget that this 'moral education'—or the organic link between the individual and society—becomes truly meaningful only through the process of democratization which is yet another aspiration of a modern society. Because it is democracy—an ethos of mutuality and reciprocity—that prevents the disruption of a delicate balance in the relationship between the individual and society. How to inculcate the ethos of democracy is, therefore, a major challenge that confronts every sensible educator in modern times. Democracy, it has to be realized, is not just about mega political events: about elections and formation of governments. Substantial democracy implies essentially a way of life: a mode of thinking, acting and engaging with the everyday world. It demands from us the ability to think and choose; it expects our critical and creative engagement and active participation in the way we manage our affairs. It also expects an *inclusive* mind—willingness to listen to others, to debate, dialogue and work together. In other words, while it demands the relative autonomy of the individual, it also requires what Habermas would have regarded as a shared 'public sphere' in which we can talk, communicate and dialogue (Pusey 1987:89). Needless to add, democracy as a way of life seeks to challenge asymmetry and authoritarianism. It demands perpetual alertness: an ability to establish the necessary linkage between the formal component of democracy(casting votes) and the rhythm of everyday life—protesting against injustice, striving for collective welfare, and overcoming our inertia and stagnation. It is important to fight for, and to retain this democratic ideal because, as history has demonstrated, societies which otherwise appear to be modern can also invite authoritarianism: be it

Stalinism or fascism. In other words, if we do not activate ourselves, if we refuse to bear the responsibility of freedom, authoritarianism becomes inevitable. As political philosophers and social psychologists have reminded us, the 'fear of freedom' can negate the very foundation of a 'sane society' (Fromm 1980). One must, therefore, learn to live with freedom: how to protect it, or how not to allow it to get degenerated into the cult of narcissism or selfishness.

Not surprisingly, educationists have given tremendous importance to the democratic ideal. It seeks to give autonomy to the learner, her participation in the learning process; it wants the learner to think, interrogate, critique and question; and it expects a more egalitarian relationship between the teacher and the taught.[4] Education, as the spirit of democratization implies, is not an exercise in passive reception of existing ideas and knowledges; it is essentially an ongoing engagement—experiencing knowledge as a continual process, not as a finished product. Paulo Freire, I would argue, has given a radical meaning to this democratic ideal (Freire 1972). Freire speaks of 'dialogic education': a system of learning and teaching that overcomes the 'culture of silence', frees itself from the 'monologistic' interpretations, and rests on mutuality, reciprocity and constant interaction between the teacher and the taught. It is different from 'banking education' which, according to Freire, is 'an act of depositing in which the students are the depositories and the teacher is the depositor' (Ibid: 55). Banking education, needless to add, imposes passivity on the learner because it is assumed that 'knowledge is a gift bestowed by those who consider themselves knowledgeable upon those whom they consider to know nothing (Ibid: 56). It is anti-democratic. It deprives the oppressed of their own language, their own struggle, their own agency. But dialogic education which Freire regards as the 'pedagogy to the oppressed' opens up a new possibility: the teacher and the taught are engaged in a joint project through which they explore the world. Freire's Marxian humanism and existentialist faith in human agency enable him to see education as a catalyst to social transformation: from silence to reflexivity, from passivity to creativity, from monologue to dialogue, and from asymmetry to symmetry. It is immensely inspiring. It prepares us to accept the challenge, and the need to strive for a kind of education that truly democratizes and decolonizes our consciousness. Indeed, Freire's message has a deeper significance. Dialogic education gives us the strength to believe in ourselves, to fight injustice and exploitation. It also helps us to humanize modernity, and rescue it from the monopoly of select experts, specialists and technocrats. Imagine a classroom in which a teacher initiates a discussion on, say, Indian democracy. And she creates an environment in which children are encouraged to come forward with their own viewpoints. It is possible that someone critiques it, and talks about child labour, poverty, starvation death, caste violence and female infanticide; someone speaks of the tyranny of majoritarianism; and someone praises it for its ability to conduct regular elections, and allow multiple political parties to exist. Imagine that she listens to all, participates in the debate as yet another equal member(maybe with little more experience), and instead of coming forward with final answers, poses new questions. Possibly the classroom would begin to radicalize itself, overcome caste/gender hierarchies, and make democracy truly meaningful—a mode of everyday existence.

Another important challenge that the age of modernity poses before us is that of secularism. It does indeed make sense when we say that modernity accelerates the process of secularization: a process through which the impact of religion on public affairs gets reduced, and scientific knowledges begin to acquire more legitimacy than, say, theological interpretations of the world. It does not, however, mean that religion withers away in a modern/secular world. Instead, it can be argued, religion modulates itself, and assumes diverse forms (Pathak 1998: 91-93). At times, it becomes merely one's 'private affair'; at times, it generates charismatic cult figures promoting multiple practices of meditation or 'art of living' campaigns; at times, it is a spiritual quest for liberation from the discontents of a technocratic/bureaucratic world; and at times, it nurtures what is now known as 'fundamentalism': an aggressive attempt to reconstruct the polity, culture and society on the basis of 'religious purity'. Yet, what is important to note is that, despite the prevalence of religion, modernity does indeed lead to the expansion of the secular space; human beings have now more opportunities to see beyond the confines of religion; and the state can function without much interference from religious institutions. Even, as our own experiences suggest, traditional religious practices and institutions like *Durga puja* and *Diwali*, and even caste practices get increasingly secularized.

The process of secularization has liberating effects. It stimulates free thinking, resists priesthood and cultural orthodoxy, and generates critical consciousness. In fact, the enthusiastic proponents of the secularization thesis may feel tempted to see religion as an obstacle to free/scientific enquiry: religion as some sort of 'collective neurosis', or an 'ideology' leading to 'false consciousness'. But it is not altogether free from ambiguities. In fact, it leads to some sort of moral and existential crisis. Nietzsche, we know, declared: 'God is dead'; and existentialist philosophers started reflecting on the 'meaninglessness' of existence in a godless world. From Camus to Heidegger to Sartre—we saw the intensity of a quest: how to cope with this 'absurdity', how to retain 'authenticity', or how to acquire the courage to carry on like Sisiphus, and not to commit suicide. Yet, as they could see, it was not easy; 'bad faith' or 'inauthenticity' would often characterize our acts and roles. Living in a godless world was no easy endeavour. Even sociology—a distinctively modern discipline—was enquiring into the implications of this ambiguous situation. Max Weber, for instance, expressed his anguish when he said that science could not provide binding norms and ideals, and a meaning to existence (Weber 1948). As Weber would have argued, it is not particularly easy to live meaningfully when one has ceased to be 'religiously musical'! And Emile Durkheim—yet another great sociologist of religion—felt, 'we are going through a stage of transition and moral mediocrity when old gods are growing old or already dead, and others are not yet born' (Durkheim 1965: 475).

Herein lies the challenge that educators have to address. Yes, secular education is the order of the day. But does it mean the death of the sacred—the end of wonder, reverence and faith? Or, is it possible to have secular education without losing the longing for the transcendent? Let us see how Durkheim coped with this challenge. He hoped that 'a day will come when our societies will know again those hours of creative effervescence, in the course of which new ideas arise and new formulae are found which serve for a while as a guide to humanity; and when hours shall have been passed through once, men will spontaneously feel the need of reliving them from time to time in thought, that is to say, of keeping alive their memory by means of celebrations which regularly reproduce their fruits' (Ibid: 475). One who has studied Durkheim carefully would admit that he was essentially hinting at the power of religious ceremonies and festivals because, for him, 'religion is something eminently social, and religious representations are collective representations which express collective realities' (Ibid: 22). No matter how modern/secular a society is, it needs to experience this moral power of the collective to save itself from disintegration or the aberrations of egotistic individualism. To be religious, for Durkheim, is not necessarily to be superstitious. Instead, as he sought to remind us, to be religious is to be moral; it is to realize the limitedness of the solitary individual, and the need to merge with the transcendent power of the collective:

> From the mere fact that society exists, there is also, outside of the individual sensations and images, a whole system of representations which enjoy marvellous properties. By means of them, men understand each other, and intelligences grasp each other. They have within them a sort of force or moral ascendancy, in virtue of which they impose themselves upon individual minds. Hence the individual at least obscurely takes account to the fact that above his private ideas, there is a world of absolute ideas ascending to which he must shape his own; he catches a glimpse of a whole intellectual kingdom in which he participates, but which is greater than him. This is the first intuition of the realms of truth (Ibid: 485).

Indeed, for him, the reverence for the sacred could be seen—if we take two examples at random—when we all stand up, and sing the national anthem, or when we assemble in a collective gathering, be it a fair or a ceremony, and forget our little identities. Not surprisingly, as I have already said, Durkheim repeatedly insisted on this moral component of education: how to enable the child to realize and internalize the power of the collective which, for him, symbolizes the sacred. Secular education should not, therefore, mean the loss of the sacred, and its implicit moral component.

Well, Durkheim gave a distinctively sociological meaning to religion. Not all believers would, however, agree with him, particularly the way he equated the sacred with the social. Even when the power of society has immense sanctity, it is possible to argue that beyond the boundaries of the clan/community/nation lies another domain of the sacred which, for example, a Vedantic philosopher would regard as the Imperishable Brahman who is 'neither gross, nor fine; neither short, nor long; ...neither shadow, nor darkness; neither air, nor space; unattached, without taste, without smell, without eyes, without ears, without breath...' (BU. III: 8.8.). In other words, Durkheim's sociology, it may be argued, is not sufficiently adequate to make sense of a far deeper quest: man's spiritual longing for the Eternal and the Absolute. Nevertheless, his significance lies in the fact that he put emphasis on some sort of 'civil religion'[5], and on the need for reverence and humility without which secular reasoning might lead to narcissism and aggression. In a way, Durkheim added some sort of ethico-religious component to Western secularism.

In a society like ours, characterized by diversity of religious beliefs and practices, the challenge of secular education acquires another important dimension. The process of secularization, its adherents assert, comes as a promise; it is a road to modernity, nation-making, development and progress. It resists the onslaught of majoritarianism, and allows plurality of traditions to co-exist. It is in this sense that our brand of secularism is often being interpreted as a practice of equal respect to all religions. In concrete terms, it means the capacity to see beyond the horizons of one's own religious culture, create an accommodative space which is open to other traditions, and generate a sense of cohesive nation working for its development.

Educationists have often spoken of this secular lesson: the need for plurality, tolerance and composite culture. In fact, if we look at independent India, a major challenge that educationists did talk about was how to inculcate in the child the spirit of plurality, tolerance and respect to multiple traditions. Not atheism, but equal respect to all religions became the primary educational agenda. No wonder, from Kabir to Nanak, from Ramakrishna to Gandhi, from Bhagat Singh to Nehru—all became secular icons(often popularized through calendar art and school texts) symbolizing cultural syncretism, religious tolerance and spiritual depth. And the Kothari Commission Report—yes, a progressive/Nehruvian document on education—revealed this spirit rather sharply:

> We suggest that a syllabus giving well-chosen information about each of the major religions should be included as a part of the course in citizenship or as part of general education to be introduced in schools and colleges up to the first degree. It should highlight the fundamental similarities in the great religions of the world and the emphasis they place on cultivation of certain broadly comparable and moral and spiritual values (Government of India 1966:21).

This accommodative spirit, we do realize, was needed for a new nation that had just passed through the trauma of partition and resultant violence. Secular education, it was thought, would help us to overcome all sorts of sectarianism and their excessive ritualism, and thereby create national unity. It was indeed an urgent political need. We do realize its gravity because one's narrow/religious identity continues to be aroused for breeding communalism: an environment of hatred and suspicion. An understanding of other religious traditions must, therefore, be seen as an important educational objective. As a teacher, I myself have realized how significant it is to inspire young learners to appreciate the deeper experience of connecting a series of revelations emanating from diverse faiths from the Sermon on the Mount to the longing of a Sufi mystic, from the experience of detachment in the *Bhagavadgita* to the Buddhist practice of overcoming pain and suffering. However, this quest ought to be authentic. It must see beyond political expediency. It must emanate from a spiritual urge to strive for an oceanic/universal feeling: an act of communion with the transcendent. It is this quest which, I believe, would give real depth and substance to secularism. Far from remaining just a state-directed activity or a lesson of strategic 'tolerance', it would enter deep inside our consciousness, and make us feel the charm of the ultimate merger—unity amidst differences. With spiritual depth secularism would become truly substantial.

To sum up, the challenge that confronts educationists in the secular age is essentially three-fold: (a) how to evolve a mode of learning that inspires the learner to question the bundle of superstitions and prejudices, promote an enquiring spirit, and invite the ever-expanding frontiers of knowledge; (b) how to see beyond sectarianism, internalize a dialogic/accommodative mind, and cultivate what Gandhi regarded as 'the habit of understanding and appreciating the doctrines of various great religions of the world in a spirit of reverence and broad-minded tolerance' (Gandhi 1953:53); and (c) how not to negate the quest for the fundamental unity of beings, and realize a deeply aesthetic/spiritual sensitivity which, I believe, Tagore expressed in a remarkably revealing fashion:

> The fact that we exist has its truth in the fact that everything else does exist, and the 'I am' in me crosses the finitude whenever it deeply realizes itself in the 'Thou art'. This crossing of the limit produces joy, the joy that we have in beauty, in love, in greatness. Self-forgetting, and in a higher degree, self-sacrifice, is our acknowledgement of our experience of the infinite. This is the philosophy which explains our joy in all arts, the arts that in their creations intensify the sense of the unity which is the unity of truth we carry within ourselves. ...Its standard of reality, the reality that has its perfect revelation in a perfection of harmony, is hurt when there is a consciousness of discord, because discord is against the fundamental unity which is in its centre (Tagore 1983a:10).

Yes, the crossing of the limit, as the poet felt, is what spiritual reverence is all about. It is also a deeply aesthetic experience—a sense of beauty and harmony. Without this wonder, an educator should realize, science becomes instrumental, politics gets reduced into a ruthless strategy, and modernity loses its depth.

III
EDUCATION IN THE CONTEXT OF THE CHANGING CULTURAL LANDSCAPE

Responsible individualism, democratic/dialogic consciousness, and union of the secular and the sacred—these three ideals, as I have just pointed out, ought to strike the imagination of an educator, particularly when societies modernize themselves. It is not, however, easy to pursue these objectives. The road is full of obstacles, temptations and sensations, and an educator needs to be aware of these challenges. In fact, as societies are becoming more and more hyper-modern and complex, new ethical questions have begun to haunt our conscience.

To begin with, I wish to reflect on modern technology which has become an integral component of our everyday living. Yes, technology, as the ethos of modernity suggests, is liberating in nature. It is through technology that the potential of theoretical sciences unfolds itself. Unlike the theories of science, it is concrete, tangible and visible. It does things, makes wonders, and gives us tools and devices to overcome the constraints imposed by nature. It is dynamic. It progresses continually, and becomes more subtle, refined, sophisticated, and even democratic. It promises emancipation from toil and servitude; it leads to the material well-being of the community. Technological progress is, therefore, seen as a hallmark of development. No wonder, policy makers have always insisted on the need to learn this technological skill, and cope with its rhythm. In fact, these days techno-scientific education has acquired the legitimacy of 'high status' knowledge[6].

But then, the ever-expanding technology, it should not be forgotten, causes serious ethical and pedagogical problems. For instance, technology can be so overwhelmingly powerful over our lives that we tend to lose critical consciousness, or the freedom to see beyond its paradigm. Technology evolves its own logic of progress. It becomes a sort of fetish, and every new piece of technological innovation is seen as 'inevitable' to which we are required to submit. In fact, technology seduces us through its well-advertised narratives of speed, efficiency and comfort. It is, therefore, not surprising that a laptop, to take a simple illustration, no longer remains just a laptop. We are told that this 'little wonder' which has been created by 'an unbeatable combination of speed and lightness' can make us free from the tiresome 'walking around with a notebook that weighs like a brick'. Finally 'a NOTEBOOK as light as a notebook' has arrived; and we are, therefore, persuaded to indulge in a truly spectacular 'digital experience':

> Welcome to Reliance Digital. 42,000 sq. ft. of world class digital experience, with the best products from across the world, right here in Gurgaon. With over 6000 products on display for you to touch, try and compare and loads of irresistible offers in store! So walk right in any day of the week and treat yourself to a truly one-of-a kind digital shopping experience! [7]

No wonder, technology causes indulgence. It becomes exceedingly difficult to come out of it. It is, therefore, not surprising that it has caused severe imbalance—acute environmental damage, loss of self-restraint and poverty of imagination. That is why, educationists need to rethink the mode of engagement with technology. Technology is liberating only when we know the art of using it: when we realize that the same mobile phone which we use to give an urgent message to a friend from a remote territory can also colonize our bodies and souls, if we become indulgent; or, not everything can be gained through the speed of a fancy car because there are moments when the poetry of rhythmic walking—walking in silence—liberates our consciousness, and makes us communicate with the tree, with the butterfly, and with the clouds in the sky. In other words, as a series of thinkers—from Gandhi to Illich, from Schumacher to Marcuse—have pointed out, it is naive to equate the depth of living with just technological comforts. It is really sad that in our times the ethos of perpetual adjustment to the changing nature of technology has become the dominant educational practice. This 'social adjustment', as Jacques Ellul has argued with great conviction, has made the other goals of liberation and individualized instruction almost meaningless. Because the technological system, as Ellul would have argued, does not work for the benefit of man, but for its own benefit. Man becomes a 'thing' to be controlled for the benefit of the system (see Spring 1972:149-72). See its consequences. These days, it would not be wrong to say, technology is causing an illusion of learning, and techniques of information seem to have acquired more importance than the entire experience of acquiring fundamental knowledge. Take, for instance, the obsessive use of the Internet, and the techno-illusion it creates: one can learn as if only when the entire information were seen on the screen! The fact is that knowledge (or knowledge enriched by wisdom) is not just information; instead, it is the ability to engage with this information, contextualize it, see it through a theoretical/ philosophical perspective, evolve a mature understanding of the world, and eventually experience it. In other words, what education requires is the cultivation of a critical/reflexive/ imaginative mind, not just a technically efficient consciousness.

It is indeed a matter of concern that even little children are using the Internet to download the information for doing all sorts of fashionable 'projects' through which schools seek to impress their adherents—mainly, the insecure parents who fear that without the Internet their children might lag behind. This obsession is damaging. Because children must touch, feel and experience the world—its vibrations, colours and activities; they must interact with people around, and learn how to observe, think and relate. In other words, if we take a simple example, it is more important for them to play football to develop physical/ motor skills, and acquire the intensity of team spirit, rather than sitting alone in a room and downloading the information on diverse places where the World Cup Soccer took place, and then writing a 'project' on this borrowed material!

True, as the enthusiastic proponents of new technology argue, there are now learning packages available for a whole range of subjects which individuals are capable of working through their own speed and at times that suit them. Well, I am aware that these days social scientists have begun to speak of the 'network society'(Barney 2004); and 'virtual communities' are seen as less hierarchical and less discriminatory, and more egalitarian and inclusive than traditional communities. So even if one does not belong to a privileged school or a social group, one can get all sorts of information and learning material from the Internet. While not entirely negating the liberating potential of the computerized learning, I am emphasizing that learning is after all a deeply enriching social experience. One learns through active engagement with real people: meeting and interacting with them, relating to teachers and fellow learners, and seeing, travelling and experiencing the world. The instantaneity of the virtual reality should not be allowed to make us forget this basic truth. We ought to realize that the dislocation and disembodiment of network communication undermine the rootedness in place and body that is necessary for a robust experience; it would further encourage withdrawl from civil engagement, and a deepening privatization of social life. What is, therefore, needed is to restore the primacy of the social over the technological in the process of learning. It ought to be seen as an urgent concern. Furthermore, as Lyotard has shown, new technology is fast altering the very purpose of knowledge; to have education, it seems, is only to have the necessary information for optimizing one's performance and market efficiency:

> The question (overt or implied) now asked by the professional student, the state, or institutions of higher education is no longer 'Is it true? But 'What use is it?' In the context of the mercantilisation of knowledge, more often than not this question is equivalent to 'Is it saleable?' And in the context of power-growth: 'Is it efficient?' (Quoted in Usher and Edwards 1994:175)

Yes, Lyotard is not wrong in his identification of the emerging trend. The obsessive use of technology is transforming the very character of a learner. One becomes a consumer of information. And the process of consumption, one is told, must be fast, efficient and technologically sleek. The more one consumes the more saleable one becomes. How often we see schools and colleges spending a huge amount of their budget for decorating their classrooms, seminar halls and libraries with latest technological gadgets. And particularly in a country like ours, you may have a private university without talented teachers, but otherwise decorated with AC classrooms, and gorgeous computer labs. Educators ought to acquire the moral courage to resist this trend, and assert that meaningful education requires patience and endurance, not instant solutions; meditative silence, not neurotic restlessness for immediate success; depth of criticality, not smartness of the market; and above all, a truly context-specific creative engagement with technology, not absolute dependence on it.

In this context it becomes important to refer to the culture of consumerism which is having its impact on the very purpose of learning. Consumerism, it goes without saying, rests on the stimulation and cultivation of desire, and this desire, let us realize, does not remain limited only to material goods and commodities; it is essentially about style, sexuality, power and a series of symbols that valorize a marketized lifestyle. There was a time when Max Weber spoke of the role of 'this worldly asceticism' in the formation of capitalism. However, capitalism has changed, and social scientists have come forward with diverse theories to make sense of this change: from production to consumption, from Fordism to post-industrialism, from self-regulating discipline to seduction. As a matter of fact, consumerism becomes an integral component of corporate capitalism which further gets legitimated through globalization and its implicit gospel of neo-liberal free market economy. As cultural theorists—from Adorno to Baudrillard—have pointed out, consumerism spreads because of the market-driven culture, its mythologies of success and power, and the all-pervasive television-mediated cultural spectacle with its constant simulation. Even though the defenders of this culture plead for vitality, market, growth and a high standard of living, the fact is that it intensifies man's aggressive urge to have more and more. No wonder, restlessness, violence, envy, jealousy and perpetual dissatisfaction become integral components of this culture. 'The gratification yielded by one consumption experience', as Bennett wrote with great insight, 'had to give in the shortest possible time to the desire for another; indeed, the ideal consumer would forego satisfaction altogether—and desire only desire' (Bennett 2001: 161).

Needless to add, a meaningful agenda of education ought to give us the light to see and realize the pathology of consumer culture, and strive for a refreshingly new and alternative mode of living. Educationists ought to take up this challenge, particularly because in our times education itself is being seen as a road to what the adherents of consumer culture regard as 'desirable'—success filled with material prosperity. No wonder, the worth of an educational institution is often decided in terms of the success rate of its 'products': how much they can earn. Are we becoming so insensitive that it does not shock us anymore when we see the distinction between an educational institution and a shop getting increasingly blurred? Are we now absolutely adjusted to such loud declarations (made by educational institutes on their achievements) as we see in huge ads in newspapers?

SUPERIOR PLACEMENTS
IIPM CLASS OF '08 PLACEMENTS HAS JUST BEGUN!!

- *Highest Package: Rs.22,00.000/- p.a.*
- *Rs.16,00,000/- p.a. for 35+ students*
- *85 + international placements*
- *Rs.5,00,000/- plus average package*
- *1850+ national placements*[8]

Education tends to become a commodity in the marketplace. These days almost every student is destined to confront the question: 'After everything said and done, how much can you earn?' This is like preparing oneself for a life that values nothing more than the power of money to buy, consume and conquer. Is it possible to resist this trend? It is difficult, extremely difficult because consumerism is deeply related to the structure of corporate capitalism, and its ethos of economic globalization. Moreover, in a country like ours that has just begun to witness the assertion of the consumptionist middle class, an alternative project runs the risk of being condemned as 'anti-modern', 'anti-development', and 'conservative'. These days we all are consumers: consumers of energy, wine, cricket and what not. But then, what else is education if it does not dare to accomplish the impossible? Educationists, therefore, must think of a new sensitivity to see beyond the seduction of consumerism. This means the light of wisdom that enables one to see the temporality of consumer culture, and experience beauty and harmony in a more enduring relationship with oneself, with the community, and with the environment. Amidst the noise and aggression of the market, it is indeed refreshing to listen to the Buddhist message:

> *There is no greater happiness*
> *Than the happiness of freedom*
> *From selfish attachments*
> *To wealth and all things worldly*
> *Impermanent and ever-changing*
> ...
> *We who possess and desire nothing*
> *Our hearts untainted by desire and greed*
> *Not caring to hoard treasures*
> *Amongst those who hoard*
> *We shall live in ever-growing happiness*
> *And shine from afar*
> *Like the bright Gods*
> *In the heaven above*
>
> (Quoted in Kaul 2007: 90-91)

As I see school children with fancy mobile phones, or young research scholars with new bikes and cars, I realize how meaningless this Buddhist message would sound to them. But then, let it be clear that this critique of consumerism does by no means suggest that I am pleading for life-negating asceticism. What I, however, wish to assert is that it is possible as well as desirable to cultivate one's inner resources, and reduce considerably the dependence on a series of false needs—or needs artificially constructed by the market and its culture industry. A school student once shared her experience of a shopping mall with me. Yes, the mall—its architecture, its technological wonders, its vibrancy—did have tremendous appeal to her mind. Yet, I could see the traces of discomfort. 'Although I liked the mall, I could not deny its artificiality'. In her remark I could see the beginning of a serious enquiry. She was not yet mature enough to understand the reason behind this artificiality; she was possibly feeling a distinction between the real and the artificial. And herein, I believe, lies the challenge before us. The task of education is to arouse a kind of aesthetic sensibility—the ability to distinguish what is enduring from what is temporal, and what is real from what is mythical. The task of education is to inculcate in the child a taste for a new and alternative notion of good living. It does not glorify poverty. Nor does it find anything heroic in one's indulgence with the 'consumer's paradise'. Instead, it values creative accomplishment, aesthetic enrichment and communitarian engagement. Or, as Erich Fromm would have reminded us, the ethical challenge confronting educationists is how to overcome the all-pervasive 'marketing character', and strive for a 'being' mode of existence which is 'to renew oneself, to grow, to flow out, to love, to transcend the prison of one's isolated ego, to be interested, and to give' (Fromm 1979:92).

The politics of culture has also acquired a new meaning in our times. It can be seen at two levels. First, we experience it within the boundaries of the nation itself. Yes, a nation, apart from its distinctive geographical/territorial location and modern polity, needs to have a shared culture: a culture evolving and emerging out of a rich civilizational memory. But then, in a multi-cultural society like ours, the process of acquiring a shared culture is extraordinarily complex. Even though the proponents of cultural syncretism—an idea that got added momentum in the process of our collective struggle for decolonization—plead for 'unity in diversity 'as the fundamental perquisite for a new nation, the fact remains, as many political sociologists apprehend, that the culture of the dominant community often becomes hegemonic, and seeks to hijack the culture of the entire nation (Oommen 1997). In its extreme form, we all know, it projects itself as the politics of 'cultural nationalism': something that goes against Nehru's 'discovery' of India or Gandhi's *Swaraj*. No wonder, the reaction to this hegemonic design manifests itself in diverse voices of protest: the assertion of subalternity and all sorts of identity politics reinforcing the claims of caste, ethnicity, region and language. While cultural nationalism is invariably centralizing, these voices of resistance tend to fragment, move towards plurality and differences, and at times, problematize the very concept of a unitary nation. Even though some social scientists in India trained in the discourses of postmodernism have begun to celebrate fragments and differences, the fact is that it is equally problematic. Is there another possibility—a possibility of cultural dialogue and fusion—that lies beyond cultural nationalism and postmodern relativism?

Second, at the global level we see yet another kind of cultural politics. It is the politics of globalization. Even though the interaction of cultures is not new, and the project of modernity has been spreading a set of universal values, the present form of globalization as some sort of 'time-space compression' is a post-Cold War phenomenon: a product of neo-liberal economy and technological spectacles. Globalization passes through transnational economic corporations, diasporic communities and proponents of hybrid identities. But it should not be forgotten that in a world which is ruthlessly unequal in terms of techno-economic and military resources, what projects itself as 'global culture' gets equated with the culture of global capitalism: a market-driven, media-induced, consumptionist spectacular culture that seeks to homogenize human aspirations through the entire apparatus of the all-pervasive culture industry. In other words, even if, as theoreticians like Roland Robertson would argue, there is a possibility of 'glocalization', i.e. the interplay of the global and the local, not all cultures acquire appropriate and dignified space in this exchange. That globalization in its present form privileges the centres of power can hardly be denied. What is, however, important to note is that as a reaction to this asymmetrical global culture, we witness the resurgence of cultural nationalism, religious revivalism, fundamentalism and even terrorism (Pathak 2006: 96-102).

In this cultural scenario an educator needs to realize the state of a young learner who finds herself in a terribly confusing milieu in which she confronts all sorts of conflicting trends simultaneously: hegemonic religious nationalism and limiting caste/ethnic identities; a seductive global culture of consumerism and exclusivist practices like Talibanism. Here is indeed a strange world in which she finds George W Bush as well as Osama bin Laden; Michael Jackson as well as Mayawati; malls as well as suicide bombers. In fact, the domain of education is being severely affected by this ongoing cultural politics. Not surprisingly then, while we see the proliferation of 'international' schools with a 'global' agenda (schools which are becoming more and more dissociated from the local culture, its language, its knowledge systems and its aspirations[9]), we also witness the assertion of segmented identities: the way school texts are being interrogated because of their 'caste' biases, or the way religious nationalists intend to restructure and redefine the entire curriculum in order to give a distinctive character to the nation[10].

Yes, under these circumstances, a young learner experiences an acute dilemma. What is right? What is wrong? What is one's identity? There seems no easy answer to these questions. Herein lies the challenge before educators. There is indeed violence in the hegemonic design of global capitalism or even cultural nationalism. It annihilates differences; it is insensitive to other voices. But then, a mind that seeks to confine itself only to an enclosed boundary in the name of caste, ethnicity and language is no less violent. When one says that one is predominantly a Dalit or a Brahmin, a Tamil or a Marathi, one tends to become ethnocentric, and radiates hatred that further segregates society. And the degree of ethnocentrism does by no means get reduced even if these identities are used for supposedly liberating causes: say, when it is asserted that one can understand the agony of a Dalit community only if one is a Dalit because everyone else is a potential traitor; or when it is said that a territory can be liberated only by separating 'alien' outsiders from 'pure' insiders. Casteism and parochialism, we must understand, are no less threatening than communalism and Americanism. What is, therefore, important is to strive for a more egalitarian, humane and inclusive educational environment that can help and cultivate what is regarded as the hermeneutic skill of understanding: understanding as a 'fusion of horizons', or understanding as an ongoing dialogic process. This requires more and more sensitivity and exposure to diverse cultures, humble interpretation and translation of multiple traditions, willingness to break stereotypes about others, and realization of profound humanism that unites the finest minds of different cultures and civilizations. It is a quest for authentic cosmopolitanism: an attempt to grow like a banyan tree, that, despite having deep roots, expands its branches in all directions. Let our classrooms nurture such banyan trees. In fact, I have often been attracted by the Upanishadic ideal of universalism. Its beauty lies in its ability to transcend differences, and experience profound oneness. How liberating it is to hear the Upanishadic prayer:

> You are the dark blue bird; you are the green (parrot) with red eyes. You are (the cloud) with the lightening in its womb. You are the seasons and the seas. Having no beginning you abide through omnipresence. (You) from whom all worlds are born (SU.IV: 4).

Indeed, this awareness of the universal radiates love, harmony and togetherness. It was this ideal which, I suppose, shaped Rabindranath Tagore's educational project: his message of merger and unity. In our times characterized by heightened cultural insecurity, anxiety and violence, every educationist ought to find a source of inspiration in the poet's philosophico-anthropological imagination—his critique of narcissistic nationalism, his discomfort with all that limits one's horizon, and his willingness to experience India as a great confluence of multiple traditions: an evolving possibility rather than a finished product.

This discussion would, however, remain incomplete without looking at yet another significant change which is taking place in our times. The assertion of women, and growing sensitivity to their struggles have made us aware of the discontents of patriarchy. We now realize how it hierarchizes our consciousness, subjugates women, and even defeats men by completely dehumanizing them. We also realize how patriarchy redefines itself in a hyper-modern world: how its power discourse, as ecofeminists revealed with absolute sharpness, is reflected in the practice of technology, in its language of domination over nature; and in corporate capitalism, particularly the way its culture of consumption often promotes the commodification and objectification of women's sexuality. In fact, as gender theorists have shown us, the construction of 'masculinity' and 'femininity' is situated in this power regime. As we are becoming aware of this politics, it is important that educators grow sensitive to this process of awakening. I believe that there are primarily two challenges. First, as educators we need to alter the politics of the classroom, and allow it to interrogate the existing gender stereotypes. This is to overcome segmentation and role stereotypes, and to encourage boys and girls to interact more meaningfully. This is like demolishing all sorts of dangerous typification—boys are 'rational', girls are 'emotional'; boys do well in football and boxing, girls in music and dance; boys opt for 'hard' sciences, girls prefer arts and humanities! In a way, what is needed is an extraordinarily creative task of redefining 'masculinity' and 'femininity'. In the process of growing up, boys need to realize that manhood need not express itself in physical aggression (which, every school teacher must have noticed, they tend to demonstrate in competitive sports, in their body language, in their subculture that isolates girls as too 'weak' to be taken seriously); nor is it a skill in being hard, detached, and objective (how often it is being reinforced through a belief that boys do not cry). Manhood, let them experience, is not separated from what makes us truly humane: our vulnerability, our softness, our prayer, and our longing for love and surrender. As a teacher, I have often realized how difficult it is for young learners to appreciate Gandhi's non-violence. The reason is not just political: whether or not non-violence is an appropriate strategy to fight injustice. Quite often, non-violence is being ridiculed as weak and feminine. It is almost taken for granted that violence as a form of protest is heroic, and it asserts the language of power. And herein lies the need for a pedagogic intervention. It is desirable to make them sensitive to the fact that Gandhi was altering gender stereotypes. He was conveying a message that there was no reason to separate courage from compassion, and resistance from prayer. Gandhi was indeed a man of a different kind: a man redefining the dominant notion of masculinity. Experiencing masculinity in this integral/humane way is a major step forward towards a new society that questions war, narcissistic nationalism and religious fundamentalism: in fact, everything that goes on in the name of masculinitst pride and honour.

Likewise, girls ought to be encouraged to realize that there is no especially demarcated/insulated feminist zone (cooking, nursing, school teaching); in fact, every domain of activity, be it politics, science, environment and child rearing, is open to all, and acquires a new meaning when it is characterized by knowledge, criticality, reflexivity and wisdom. In other words, girls and boys stand on the same platform; and it is our shared humanism that unites them. Education can indeed prove to be enabling, and show, as Simone de Beauvoir once revealed, that biology, unlike what Sigmund Freud said, is not destiny, and women are by no means the weaker sex. And even the notion of the 'weaker sex' is problematic. A reflexive pedagogy must interrogate this, and make us rethink. Was Gandhi complete without Kasturba, or Vivekananda without his mother? Possibly it is possible to teach history or political biography in a different manner so that it enters the zone of silence, and brings female voices: women's narratives, experiences and struggles in the domain of knowledge. Only then is it possible to contest a series of oppressive ideas we take for granted: men make history, and women do not deserve to be recorded in the documents of public history. The point that I am trying to plead for is that we need to work on school curriculum, teaching practices, orientation of teachers, and pedagogic experimentations to take education to a higher level of maturity so that it can be conducive to the changes taking place in our times.[11]

Second, I believe that we also need to see beyond the existing hierarchy of knowledges and human faculties. It is unfortunate that the legacy of what can broadly be regarded as Baconian/

Cartesian science continues to prevail, and objective/rational/ scientific orientation is often being associated with men, and 'femininity' being equated with 'inferior' faculties like subjectivist/particularist/ emotional thinking. This duality, and simultaneous privileging of the so-called masculinist/logical/ linear reasoning, I would argue, have fractured and fragmented human consciousness, and caused a terribly violent relationship between man and woman, and man and nature. What we, therefore, need is to resist this epistemological violence (Cartesian duality of body and mind, Baconian domination over 'feminine' nature, and positivistic science leading to depersonalization and fragmentation of the self of the knower), and move towards a more humane/integral thinking that evolves a point of mediation between reason and emotion, objectivity and subjectivity, and science and art. In fact, the increasing enrolment of girls as such is not a sufficient condition for liberating our consciousness. Unless we think, feel and experience the world in a qualitatively different way, the violence of patriarchy would continue to prevail. What is, therefore, important is to see the discontents of the so-called masculinist knowledge—particularly, its heavy emphasis on cognitive/objective rationality and reductive explanation, and instead appreciate the possibility of what Hilary Rose with her profound gender sensitivity regards as 'thinking from caring' which derives its inspiration from inter-connectedness, holism and harmonious relationship with nature (Rose 1994:28-50). To put it in concrete terms, let a young learner begin to realize that science and poetry, mathematics and music, economics and anthropology, logic and compassion, and reason and intuition need not be seen as distinct and separate. Instead, the continual interplay of disciplines and diverse faculties of knowledge creates a more holistic, humane and gender-sensitive orientation to the world.

IV
KEEPING THE QUEST ALIVE

Education, as we are arguing, is not just for mere utility; it has a higher significance; it should transform our consciousness, widen our horizon, make us sensitive, and create a society that values harmony, compassion and egalitarianism. Yet, a disturbing question haunts us: do these ideals really matter in a society that is terribly violent and pragmatic—a society that tends to reduce everything into the logic of money, a society in which, it would not be wrong to say, every child gets a message that education has no other significance except its market value? Before we come forward with any feasible answer, it is important to examine how as a civilization or as a modern nation or as a market economy we responded to these issues.

Indeed, as we look at our civilization we see a continual reflection on these ideals. Where else does one find such a striking emphasis on the difference that the ancient sages made between *vidya* and *avidya*? Yes, *vidya*, it was repeatedly asserted, does by no means mean mere knowledge of the phenomenal world; instead, it is essentially a penetrating journey to the inner world—an awareness and realization of the transcendent Reality, the Ultimate Truth:

> ....Verily, not for the sake of the beings are the beings dear but the beings are dear for the sake of the Self. Verily, not for the sake of all is all dear but all is dear for the sake of the Self. Verily, ... it is the Self that should be seen, heard of, reflected on and meditated upon. Verily, by the seeing of, by the hearing of, by the thinking of, by the understanding of the Self, all this is known' (BU. II: 4.5).

In the absence of this knowledge everything else becomes secondary or *avidya* which causes error and leads to falsehood and illusions. This emphasis on the ultimate knowledge—which is not cognitive/technical, but essentially intuitive/spiritual—has led to a profound philosophic debate on the nature and status of the empirical reality that we comprehend through sense organs. Can it actually understand the Absolute and the Eternal? We are told:

> You cannot see the seer of seeing, you cannot hear the hearer of hearing, you cannot think the thinker of thinking, you cannot understand the understander of understanding. He is your Self which is in all things. Everything else is evil (BU.III:4.2).

What does it mean? Does it suggest that the empirical world with all its forms and variations, or the world that we see, touch and hear is unreal: merely a play, a dream, a mirage? Look at the way Samkara—a great sage philosopher—continued the Vedantic tradition, and further contributed to the debate. As the magician is not at any time affected by the magical effect produced by himself because it is unreal, so the highest Self, said Samkara, is not affected by the world. In other words, the complete comprehension of the Brahman is the highest end of man, since it destroys the root of all evils such as ignorance, the seed of the entire *Samsara*. And the Brahman is eternal, all-knowing, absolutely self-sufficient, ever pure, intelligent and free, pure knowledge and absolute bliss. Does it then mean that the world has to be rejected? Even Samkara, it seems, would not suggest such an extreme proposition. Possibly it only means that the empirical world cannot exist by itself. It is wholly dependent on the Brahman. In other words, without an awareness of the linkage between the temporal and the transcendental, the finite and the infinite, the discrete ego and the Universal Self, the world becomes a source of servitude and bondage. And what is, therefore, needed is not the negation of the world, but a creative engagement with it: an urge to overcome its finitude and limitedness, and take it to a higher level of merger. It is like realizing: 'As the flowing rivers disappear in the sea, having lost their name and form, thus a wise man freed from name and form goes to the divine Person who is greater than the great'.

I am not referring to this debate merely because of academic curiosity. This debate, I suppose, has a continuity, and what is interesting is that it has shaped even some of the illuminating discourses on education which emerged in India in modern times. It is in this context that I wish to recall the contributions of Sri Aurobindo, Rabindranath Tagore and Mohandas Karamchand Gandhi. Yes, all of them were 'modern' in a sense that they grew up in an environment that emerged out of post-Enlightenment developments in the world; they experienced colonialism, the triumph of modern science and technology, and above all, an extremely powerful doctrine of social evolution and material progress. They knew that one could not regress to a mythical past, and the new world ought to be coped with. But then, all of them felt that the flow of civilization should be seen as an ongoing living tradition capable of redefining itself time and again. It was, therefore, not surprising that all of them came forward with a refreshingly new possibility—not conservative revivalism, but a meaningful alternative. True, it was felt that modern education with its secular orientation and its emphasis on new scientific knowledges relating to the tangible/phenomenal world must be negotiated with. Yet, Macaulay's colonial arrogance, his utter contempt for our civilization, and, for that matter, the decline in the spiritual/aesthetic quest because of heavy emphasis on the externalities of life, they felt, must be fought, and a new kind of education—modern, yet in tune with finer aesthetic spiritual aspirations—should emerge.

Sri Aurobindo, for instance, had a deep understanding of the process of social evolution. He could see the arrival of the age of reason and its implicit possibilities: how it is 'an advance upon the comparative immobility and slow subconscient or half-conscient evolution of infrarational societies' (Sri Aurobindo 1977:201-02). Yet, the age of reason with its liberal democracy or state socialism could not be the ultimate destiny of humankind because 'reason is neither the first principle of life, nor can be its last, supreme and sufficient principle' (Ibid: 202). He felt that we were destined to evolve further, and move towards a new spiritual age. He examined the discontents of the age of reason—say, how the cult of 'individualistic democratic freedom' promotes intense competition and a high degree of egotism, and eventually results in 'the survival not of the spiritually, rationally or physically fittest, but of the most fortunate and vitally successful' (Ibid: 186). Or, for that matter, state socialism with its 'collectivist mystique' would not be able to overcome the limits of individualistic democracy because it too degenerates, negates human creativity, and leads to 'complete unanimity of mind, speech, feeling and life' (Ibid: 193). We, therefore, need to see beyond the parameters of reason, experience the spiritual oneness of being, and arrive at a new age in which inner freedom and art of relatedness go together. 'No machinery invented by the reason', wrote Sri Aurobindo, 'can perfect either the individual or the collective man; an inner change is needed in human nature'. (Ibid: 207). Not surprisingly, Sri Aurobindo gave a new meaning to education. It should enable the individual to grow, cultivate a sense of profound freedom, and sharpen the physical, vital, mental and psychic states of being:

> It will hold sacred all the different parts of man's life which correspond to the parts of his being, all his physical, vital, dynamic, emotional, aesthetic, ethical, intellectual, psychic evolution, and see in them instruments for growth towards a diviner being. (Ibid: 213).

With this objective Sri Aurobindo suggested concrete pedagogical proposals. He was against all sorts of imposition and forceful learning. 'Nothing', he felt, 'can be taught'. The teacher is primarily a catalyst—a helper who encourages the child to realize her potential, and develop the faculties of learning—how to observe, compare, remember and judge, or how to become aware of the 'psychic' centre of one's being, and realize a sense of universality, limitless expansion and timeless continuity.

Likewise, Rabindranath Tagore, as I have already indicated, loathed finitude and fragmentation: the way school as a learning machine with its regimentation crushes the soul of the child. For Tagore, man ought to see beyond mere utility, realize 'that surplus which ever overflows the boundaries of the immediate time and space, restlessly pursuing its adventure of expression in the varied form of self-realization' (Tagore 1983a:9), and experience a sense of vastness and universalism, and learn through a creative merger with nature by appreciating not just analytical reason, but also aesthetic and spiritual sensibilities.

True, Tagore saw the virtues of the modern age: its spirit of enquiry and scientific discoveries. Yet, with his poetic sensibility he could also see the discontents of modernity—its violence and aggression, its ruthless mechanization and dissociation from the flow of natural life. He could listen to 'the cry of the oppressed spirit of man which struggles to free itself from the grip of screws and bolts, of unmeaning obsessions' (Ibid: 3). Education, he felt, must play a key role in liberating us, and transforming our consciousness and orientations. He was a poet. He was also a practical doer. His experimentations sought to show us the domain of possibilities.

And finally, Mohandas Karamchand Gandhi pleaded for 'basic' or 'integral' education in order to restore the dignity of labour, and unite the mind and the body, and productive work and theoretical articulations. This sort of education, he felt, would decolonize and debrahaminize our consciousness, fight elitism and duality in our society, and take us nearer to his dream of *swaraj*: a new society based on decentralization, austerity, ahimsa and self-sufficiency. Essentially Gandhi wanted to take education nearer to people: their local knowledges, their productive experiences and their needs. He was not an educationist—the way Tagore was. Yet, the central message he conveyed—the principle of learning through doing, the unity of theory and practice, and the purification of human consciousness through productive labour—did have its appeal to many educationists. Even when there were subtle differences amongst these great minds(Sri Aurobindo put emphasis on spiritual awakening, Tagore on aesthetic sensibility, and Gandhi on productive labour), what united them was their firm conviction that education ought to be endowed with a deeper significance. It is not just for learning a 'skill' or earning one's livelihood. It is essentially for creating a new being: intellectually mature, aesthetically sensitive, spiritually developed, and determined to create a world that values the sprit of trust, care, reciprocity, freedom and universalism. And it is for a new society free from fragmentation, alienation and violence.

In fact, even at a time when our political freedom from colonialism led to the 'practicality' of nation-making project, the higher objectives of education were recalled, and moral/ ethical questions were not altogether forgotten. A newly independent nation like ours, it was felt, must overcome the trauma of partition—the violence implicit in communal politics, renew its dialogic space, and consolidate its syncretic culture. Furthermore, it was believed that we must build up the solid base—techno-scientific infrastructure—for development and progress in order to survive in the new world. It was, therefore, not surprising that the idea of a new citizen—democratic, secular, scientifically oriented, and having a pan-Indian national identity—gained widespread legitimacy. Jawaharlal Nehru—the architect of this project—did emphasize the role of 'scientific temper', and almost all education commission recommendations which were influenced by this grand project attached a new meaning to education (Pathak 2002: 94-101). It must cultivate a scientific temper, consolidate secularism and a composite culture, fight 'parochial' identities, and strengthen the spirit of Indianess:

> The common core will include the history of India's freedom movement, the constitutional obligations and other content essential to nurture national identity. These elements will cut across subject areas and will be designed to promote values such as India's common cultural heritage, egalitarianism, democracy and secularism, equality of the sexes, protection of the environment, removal of social barriers, observance of the small family norm and inculcation of the scientific temper. All educational programmes will be carried on in strict conformity with secular values (The New Education Policy in Shukla 1988:4-5).

Even if, because of the class composition of the ruling elite, and lack of political will, the state failed to fulfil its promise, there was still some sort of conscience in our collective imagination. Equality, common schooling, social justice: these ideals did not wither away completely. Things, however, began to change. Nationalism itself became a contested domain; we witnessed the assertion of cultural nationalists. They interrogated the doctrine of secular nationalism, regarded it as 'pseudo secular', and alleged that it had a tendency to pamper 'minoritism', and negate 'Hindu' traditions. No wonder, they took active interest in education, and their focus, as we saw, got shifted from Nehruvian secularism to 'Hinduization' of consciousness, from Tagore's aesthetic sensibility to a kind of regimented training for creating a Hindu *rashtra*, from Gandhi's linkage with the masses through productive vocationalism to a set of hierarchical practices, and from Sri Aurobindo's spiritual awakening to religion as an ideology of aggressive nationalism. It led to a culture of hatred and suspicion. It was anti-dialogic. Education began to lose its finer ideals.

From the doctrine of cultural nationalism to the neo-liberal agenda of economic globalization—it was not a long journey. In the post-socialist era, as the march of global capitalism appeared to be irresistible, it found its adherents not just from the rightist forces(they are happy to unite Hindu nationalism with global capitalism), but also from the centrist and even the 'leftist' forces. In a way, it became the ruling ideology, and it changed the entire discourse of education. We are seeing its implications. Far from remembering aesthetic/political/democratic ideals of education, we are now comfortable with the idea of 'knowledge capital' to reap the benefits of a 'rapidly growing economy'. Because, as the National Knowledge Commission states without any ambiguity, what India needs is the 'development of a skilled and educated workforce' (2007:14). Yes, the message is clear. Education must become a 'skill' to fulfil the demands of the market.

What matters now is just the packaging of education as a saleable commodity. There are primarily two reasons for this changing scenario. First, the market itself began requiring educational credentials as a precondition of employment. As a result, schools are now viewed more in terms of an 'opportunity' to meet the demands of the market. Second, the ongoing explosion of commodities, with newer commodities entering the market every day, radically alters the picture of secular salvation. It is like believing that happiness stems from people's ability to satisfy their ever-expanding scope of wants. And schools contribute to the enforcement of a market society by helping people establish their levels of expectations relative to the patterns of consumption. An educationist has captured this process quite brilliantly:

> ...I enter this world under the impress of the law of scarcity. I am born as a raw material without immediate use-value to the market. This condition poses a threat to me in a market society. I need use-value to exchange on the market in order to meet

> all of my other needs. In a market society my survival depends upon this exchange. Therefore, I learn to need use-value... I learn to *need* school for my acquisition of use-value. As a child of this contemporary age of mass media, mass production and mass consumption, television advertising and the toy industry will have already taught me to associate my happiness with the consumption of market commodities.... School contributes to the formation of this conscience through the calculus of meritocracy. According to this accounting system, I must exhibit faith in the axiom that the number of years of schooling that I consume, multiplied by my level of performance/compliance as measured by my grades and standardized test scores that determine my placement within the hierarchy of the school's differentiated curriculum, will determine my use-value and, therefore, how much I can expect to gain from the market in exchange for the deployment of that use-value—my labour (Gabbard 2003: 6-7).

And this leads to terrible stress and anxiety—almost a neurotic obsession with 'success'. Look at the mood of our times. My continual interaction with school children has taught me that these days physics, to take a revealing example, is seldom experienced for its wonder and joy that ought to characterize someone who loves science, its theoretical exploration, and its luminaries like Newton, Bohr and Einstein. Instead, it is now merely a set of puzzles that one must learn to solve (by joining immensely costly coaching classes) in order to enter the lucrative techno-corporate world. Or, for that matter, economics as a body of knowledge, it seems, is only for having a career in trade, commerce and management. And whatever does not sell, be it literature or philosophy, is to be avoided or studied with a sense of utter disgust and defeat. Critical consciousness, creative exploration and aesthetic joy—these experiences tend to become outdated, and right from nursery classes one is asked to run faster, defeat others, and 'succeed' in life. Education is now devoid of all finer ideals.

This is not to suggest that a puritan notion of education devoid of all practical/worldly considerations has to be pleaded for. Doubtless, it is absolutely important to find one's vocation, earn one's livelihood, and contribute to the material well-being of society. However, when the market becomes the sole determinant, the meaning of vocation (which, as I have already indicated, is an integral component of education) undergoes dramatic changes. It becomes merely an occupation—a profitable occupation. One's subjectivity, freedom and inner calling become secondary, and the calculative logic of the market colonizes one's life-world. It is a shift from inner satisfaction to hard bargaining, from meaningfulness to utility. Moreover, it is wrong to reduce 'skill learning' into a fetish. After all, how one uses it depends on one's political/aesthetic/critical consciousness. It is like asking a simple, yet meaningfully embarrassing question: What does one do with the 'managerial skill' one acquires from a business school? Does one use it for selling wine, and thereby enhancing the profit rate of a transnational corporation? Or, does one use it for revitalizing the village panchayat so that it can tap its local resources to construct roads, schools and dispensaries? In fact, speaking of 'knowledge capital' and 'skill learning' without referring to fundamental politico-ethical questions is like allowing the alliance of technocracy and corporate capitalism to give the final judgment on what is worth learning and what is not. At a time when global capitalism seduces the rising middle class, market becomes a new religion; and it becomes exceedingly difficult to think of any other meaning of education. This difficulty gets further intensified because the prevalent techno-positivistic culture erects a wall between fact and value, information and awareness, skill and moral sensitivity, and cognition and action. It is like arguing that history, physics, economics, literature—in fact, everything—can be learned as a mere fact, a technical skill, and a set of axioms and theoretical explorations, but dissociated from inner experiences, from the journey of the self, and from ethics and politics. Fighting all these constraints is no easy proposition. But then, no revolution is possible without human praxis, without small/humble efforts. As educators, we can at least think of making a difference in our own domains of work. We need to realize the potential of a reflexive/critical pedagogy. Let us convey a message to young learners: even when they learn formal academic disciplines they can alter their meanings, radicalize their experiences, and bring education closer to the depth of life.

NOTES

1. Any careful observer of the prevalent educational scenario would find the all-pervasive presence of the rationale of the market in the domain of learning. In fact, this utilitarian appropriation of education is being legitimated through the narratives of 'success' schools/universities propagate to make their presence felt. Take, for instance, the way a private university that has just established its campus in Meerut advertises itself in a leading newspaper:

   Shobhit University stands for going beyond the established standards, and nurtures technocrats and managers so that they have a global vision and insight in their chosen fields, and are globally employable in emerging areas with special focus on 21st century professional requirements.

   Not solely that. The university appears to be so confident that it assumes that one day its 'successful' products would invariably express their gratitude by conveying a message: 'WE THANK YOU—YOU PLACE US'.
2. I have referred to Gandhi and Marx because their life-practices and philosophies were immensely illuminating for any educator. Gandhi was by no means a conservative traditionalist, despite the fact that he used to regard himself as a 'sanatani Hindu'. He was perpetually experimenting with Hinduism, and evolving critiques of many traditional practices. This critique did not emerge out of cynicism. Instead, he was positively striving for decolonization, and a non-violent/decentralized society. Likewise, Marx was not just critiquing the capitalist order; he was also visualizing an emancipatory society. Both Gandhi and Marx, I would argue, taught us a great pedagogic lesson: *when critical consciousness is endowed with love and longing for a just society, it does wonders.*
3. It is indeed unfortunate that we are witnessing a standardization of career pursuits. How often we see school students refusing (or not being encouraged) to appreciate their own specificities, and, like David Riesman's 'other-directed' beings, striving for what 'everybody' else is doing. The motto is—pursue science, and try to become a doctor, an engineer, or a management/IT professional. In their imagination everything else, it seems, is meaningless.
4. In this context it is important to note that Karl Mannheim—a great sociologist who reflected on modern times and the process of

social transformation—showed remarkable sensitivity to the democratic ideal of education. He felt the need for a broader experience of education to generate a creative bond between the teacher and the taught. A teacher as an 'authoritarian instructor' did not fascinate him; a teacher, he felt, should be 'a guide who relies upon the initiative of the learner and recognizes that for good intellectual learning a prior condition is emotional respect between the teacher and the pupil'. With the greater participation of the student in the learning process, as he felt, 'the incentives upon which learning is built will tend to move from constraints, external rewards like marks, prizes, ranking, towards mobilizing interest' (Mannheim and Stewart 1962: 19-31).

5. Even though Robert Bellah (1970) popularized the concept of 'civil religion', its roots could be found in Durkheim. Because civil religion is based on the belief of people that the foundation of their society is somehow part of a divine scheme of things. In a way, almost in a Durkheimian fashion, civil religion becomes a set of values associated with sacred symbols (say, national anthem/national flag) which are integrated into the broader society. It makes sacred certain secular values of society, and helps integrate the citizens into a national community.
6. In this context Michael Apple's work (1979) becomes relevant. Even though he referred to the sociology of American schools, his insights are no less relevant for us. For Apple, techno-scientific knowledge has acquired a 'high status' in contemporary times because of its close relationship with the corporate economy. It is seen as 'macro-economically beneficial in terms of long run benefits to the most powerful classes in society'.
7. This particular advertisement of Reliance Digital was published in the New Delhi edition of *The Hindustan Times* (16/03/08).
8. This particular advertisement was published in the New Delhi edition of *The Indian Express* (04/03/08).
9. The emergence of 'global/international' schools in our leading cities is a fact none can deny. These schools, needless to add, are completely separated from the flow of everyday life in Indian society: its climate, its culture, its struggles and its aspirations. Take, for instance, the way *G.D.Goenka World School* in Gurgaon—'a fully air-conditioned school with a superbly appointed 60 acre campus'—projects itself in a gorgeous ad published in the New Delhi edition of *The Indian Express* (04/03/08):
   - *17 acre, 5 hole trainer golf course and Equestrian centre.*
   - *400 metre athletics track, 8 playing fields for cricket, tennis, basketball, squash courts etc.*

- *Indoor swimming pools*
- *Fully equipped Fitness Centre with hi-tech Gym and Spa (steam-sauna), hair and skin care salon*
- *Multi purpose hall and Amphitheatre*
- *Deluxe air-conditioned buses for day boarders plying to Delhi, Gurgaon and Faridabad.*

10. We are living at a time when caste and religion are playing important roles in defining our identities. For example, the assertion of marginalized castes has led to a high degree of sensitivity. Its adherents interrogate dominant ideologies, strive for counter-hegemony, and examine whether our knowledge systems—say, school texts— continue to privilege forward caste perspectives, and hence undermine their own contributions. It is like asking whether school history, because of its preoccupation with Gandhi, Nehru and Indian National Congress, gives due space to the contributions made by people like Narayana Guru, Jotirao Phule and B.R. Ambedkar. At the same time, we have witnessed the assertion of religious nationalism. Its enthusiastic proponents seek to rewrite school texts, delete 'objectionable' elements that degrade 'Hindu' sentiments, and emphasize the role played by their celebrated icons, like Shivaji and Savarkar. As a matter of fact, time and again we witness this heated debate, interference in the arena of learning, and resultant violence. Indeed, the politics of identities has entered deep into the process of production and transmission of knowledge.
11. This is indeed a challenging task. Because socialization practices in patriarchal families have immense impact on the formation of identities, it is not easy for schools—even the most progressive ones—to alter these personality traits which children inherit from their families. Yet, if schools seek to retain their relative autonomy, it is important to create alternative values. Possibly, three things can be done: (a) Educators need to educate themselves. In other words, teachers need to be encouraged to reflect on their own biases. They need to unlearn many patriarchal values they themselves have inherited; (b) A new approach to the curriculum needs to be evolved. Women's narratives and experiences should enrich children's understanding of history, economics, mathematics, or any other branch of knowledge; and (c) Special tasks should be assigned without gender biases. For example, boys many be asked to perform 'soft' duties—say, giving bouquet to the Chief Guest in the school function, and girls may be engaged in a 'hard' task—say, taking care of the audio-visual system of the auditorium in which the function is taking place!

Chapter II

Exploring Reflexive Pedagogy: Towards a Radical Transformation of Schooling

It is possible to have an altogether different sensitivity to pedagogy—something that overcomes the existing dualities: formal vs. informal, rational vs. experiential, and intellectual vs. emotional. With this sensitivity we can transform the entire process of learning: from a detached/impersonal exercise in mere intellectual cognition to a deeply humane and integral experience of creative exploration. I wish to suggest that there are two central characteristics of this new pedagogy. First, it is *reflexive* because it invites the 'self' of the learner. While one learns by looking at the world out there, it is equally important to look at oneself, and continually reflect on the dynamic relationship between the knower and the known. Knowing the world out there, and knowing oneself, therefore, become two sides of the same coin. Needless to add, this art of learning ought to awaken the 'self' of the learner, arouse her sensitivity, and make her think, feel, wonder and suffer. Second, with this reflexivity, it is hoped, would begin a sense of *compassion*: a creative bond with the world. Knowing the world, let us realize, is not just theorizing, explaining and controlling it; knowing the world is also about understanding and loving it. In this sense the kind of pedagogy we are talking about does not fall into the Cartesian category of disembodied rationality. Instead, it is a kind of learning that values empathy and caring. And I would argue that every branch of school knowledge, be it physics or literature, mathematics or history, can be enriched by this new sensitivity. In this chapter I wish to narrate this art of learning, and also explore the obstacles that confront it.

I
THE ART OF SCIENCE

Let us begin with science education. Yes, the very word 'science' seems to have its magic. Its cognitive aura is indeed remarkable. In fact, it was Robert Merton who further popularized a highly idealized or heroic notion of science in terms of four norms, or 'institutional imperatives'—*universalism* (science transcends the barriers of time and space), *communism* (science is democratic and transparent, and hence it is a body of public knowledge), *disinterestedness* (science is being pursued for its own sake, not for any personal interest of the scientist), and *organized skepticism* (science questions everything; it does not preserve the cleavage between the sacred and profane) (Merton 1972). No wonder, science is often being seen as a clear, focused and defined road to truth—with its objectivity and empiricism, and rationality and dispassionate analysis. It is in this sense that science is said to have immense legitimacy. We do talk about scientific socialism, scientific management and even scientific motherhood! To put it otherwise, any organized/systematic/objective pursuit tends to be regarded as science. But then, apart from this generalized usage, science has also a specific connotation in formal sites of learning—particularly, when we talk about natural and life sciences like physics, chemistry and biology, and distinguish these branches of knowledge from liberal arts and humanities. As a matter of fact, schools, colleges and universities—all modern sites of learning—often retain this boundary. Disseminating science, for all practical purposes, amounts to disseminating natural and life sciences. Even though there are social sciences, these are seen to be 'soft'—not capable of occupying the status of 'hard' sciences! A possible reason behind this structure of knowledge is that the age of modernity characterized by scientific/industrial revolution witnessed immense progress—often a linear/cumulative progress—in the domain of natural and life sciences, and this progress, it was thought, would further legitimize the modernist quest for human supremacy over nature. Science—with its Bacon and Descartes, Newton and Darwin—became the most legitimate knowledge. Furthermore, as the cult of specialization with its disciplinary boundaries became more and more legitimate because of the epistemology of reductionism, natural and life sciences began to get increasingly dissociated from deeper cultural and philosophical queries.[1]

Not surprisingly, for a school child, science education means essentially a training in 'hard' science—basic and elementary physics, chemistry and biology. It has two dimensions that appeal to a learner. First, its *cognitive* component—understanding the laws of nature, and explaining natural phenomena through established paradigms and theories—is quite appealing. It gives one the power to demystify nature, and have mastery over it. Second, its *utilitarian* component—application of these basic theoretical principles for constructing technologies leading to material progress in society—gives science education a special status. Its gains are thought to be concrete, tangible and visible. No wonder, science education acquires a privileged status in all modern societies in which science is a kind of secular theology, and technologists are its celebrated champions.

In India too all major education commissions, be it the Radhakrishnan Commission (1944), or the Kothari Commission (1966), or the New Education Policy (1986), attached great importance to science education. Science, it was felt, would be needed for productivity, self-sufficiency in food, economic growth and employment. It was further argued that science must enable the learner to understand its basic principles, to develop problem-solving analytical skills, and the ability to apply them to the problems of the material environment and social change. To put it otherwise, science, it was thought, would characterize the new nation: a nation eager to develop, modernize and industrialize.

It is in this context that I wish to look at the state of science education at our schools (I mean the schools where some amount of teaching takes place). Its three salient features can be identified as follows:

(a) Yes, elementary science, as school texts tend to indicate, begins with natural wonder and curiosity. How do we make sense of the world around us? What is matter? How is it constituted? What is sound? Why do we hear it? What is electricity? Or magnetism? How do we see colours? And so on and so forth. Not surprisingly, matter and its elements, sound, light, electricity, magnetism, force, motion, heat and energy constitute the core of elementary physics that school texts prescribe. Likewise, chemistry begins with an understanding of mixture and compound, and diverse chemical formulations and equations. Or, for that matter, school biology is about life processes—not just about human body, its organism and functions, but also about plants and animals. The entire corpus of knowledge is taught in terms of a set of principles, theories and axioms which are thought to be abstract and universal, and which explain a large number of phenomena, say, right from the formation of rainbows to the functioning of the steam engine and conversion of energy. It cannot be denied that these explanatory principles help the young learner overcome the constraints of 'commonsense' and 'taken for granted' knowledges, and also enable them to celebrate reason, and think logically and coherently. Yes, for a curious young learner who has just begun to study science, it is indeed a wonderful feeling to acquire the cognitive power to explain, say, why in a thunderstorm one sees the lightening first and then hear the thunder; why in space astronauts must communicate using radio waves instead of sound waves; or why the cycle of day and night continues to recur. From Newton's law of gravitation to Dalton's theory of atoms—science, it can be said, is received (at least by those who are interested in it) with a sense of empowerment. At this juncture, it would not be inappropriate to quote a student of science who responded to my query with deep enthusiasm:

> Without science it is hard to imagine my existence. When I was in standard IX, my favourite subjects were mathematics and chemistry. Moreover, science helps one to understand the mechanism of the Earth; students come to know about many chemical solutions which we use in everyday life. Laws of motion, gravitation and many such chapters help us to understand the universe. I like science.[2]

Furthermore, these principles are taught in terms of numerical puzzles. This is like seeing the mathematical precision of science. Imagine a child being asked to solve the following numericals:

(*i*) A car weighing 1,000 kg moves at a speed of 30 m/s. When brakes are applied, the car decelerates uniformly and stops after covering a distance of 50 m. Calculate the work done by the brake. Also calculate the force exerted on the car to stop it.

(*ii*) A 100-W bulb is used for five hours. How much energy is consumed by the bulb?

Yes, school science texts (for relatively higher classes) are full of numericals of this kind which seek to convey a significant message to the child: science must avoid all sorts of vagueness; it is about measurement, quantification and precision. No wonder, in the process of growing up, learning science, for a child, is almost like acquiring immense cognitive power: how to demystify and explain (Mummy, you have been doing it for years. But still you do not know why it is quicker to boil an egg in salty water than in ordinary water); how to overcome age-old superstitions and prejudices (explaining solar and lunar eclipses in terms of the rotation of the moon and the earth, and thereby rejecting the idea of the determining divine force); and how to speak a new esoteric language that lay people do not understand. Yes, science is equated with reason, objectivity, universality, mathematical precision, specialized vocabulary and intellectual sophistication.

(b) Another major component of science teaching is what is popularly known as 'practicals'. In other words, children are expected to go to labs, learn how to use scientific instruments, and then experiment, and empirically demonstrate the validity of theoretical postulates. This is like, to take simple illustrations from practical classes, using a balance, and measuring even a fragment of a gram; or using a bar magnet, iron fillings, paper and a brush, and then measuring its magnetic field. One learns how to mix a chemical compound with the required acid, heat it, and eventually identify its exact composition, or how to dissect a frog or a rat, and see its diverse organs and parts. Wearing the lab coat, handling the instruments, observing, testing, measuring and eventually documenting everything about a successful experiment in lab manuals, for a child, is a great experience:

> *As I love studying science, so whenever I go to the lab, I get excited. Experiments help us to understand the theory better, and we get practical illustrations. I love doing experiments and questioning the conclusions.*[3]

It is like internalizing the aura of science—its experimental character, and I would also add, the kind of isolation it demands from the flow of everyday life. A lab has indeed a deeper meaning. It is a specially designed space insulated from the 'impurity' of the world. Doing experiments in the lab is, therefore, not just learning pieces of physics, chemistry and biology; it is the beginning of an effort to inculcate the principles of objectification, abstraction and detachment which science seeks to privilege.

(c) Despite the theoretical/experimental orientation I have just referred to, it cannot be denied that science, for many, is being received essentially as an utilitarian package: the way a young learner is persuaded to see a concrete and tangible relationship between science and career. Science education, it is thought, is predominantly a training for entering the techno-corporate world. In a country like ours, characterized by acute job anxiety and insecurity, science emerges as a promise—something that might enable one to find an appropriate profession, earn one's livelihood, and have some sort of social and financial security. This possibly explains almost an obsessive craze for the science stream; parental/peer group pressure, and middle class anxiety for success and security—anyone who has interacted with school children knows—compel them to opt for science. No wonder, this pragmatism transforms the entire meaning of science education. Science, an average young learner soon realizes, has to be studied not necessarily for its joy, excitement and quest for truth, but primarily for preparing herself for a series of entrance tests for medical/engineering and other professional courses. It would not be entirely wrong to say that in our country the rationale of these courses—

particularly the logic of IIT Joint Entrance Examination—has colonized the mindset of science students. Private tutors, coaching classes and specially designed guide books containing the mathematical quizzes relating to physics, chemistry and biology (in fact, this is a huge industry revealing the terrible marketization of education) begin to deprive children (even if there are remarkable exceptions who seek to pursue science for its fundamental queries) from experiencing what some of its illuminaries celebrated: critical consciousness and commitment to truth. This utter utilitarianism, I guess, might have disturbed some devoted teachers who love science, and want children to inculcate its spirit of critical enquiry.

India, it is believed, has not done so badly in science. Our expanding scientific manpower, our flourishing labs and institutes of technology, and our recent success in software engineering, it is argued, indicate the potentiality of science education. Yet, as I wish to argue, these achievements notwithstanding, there are problems with the prevalent pedagogy. In its present form science education tends to encourage some sort of mental snobbery; moreover, it creates a technical and engineering mindset, not necessarily a critical/reflexive/sensitive orientation to the world. It is in his context that I wish to suggest alternative modes of science teaching.

Science as commitment

Science, it ought to be communicated to the young learner, is not just about a set of axioms, theories, laws and their technological utility. Science is also about fundamental values. One such value is, of course, commitment—yet, commitment to a quest, to a difficult and tedious journey. Without this commitment how can one interrogate, fight the tyranny of prevalent paradigms, and propose new ideas? And this commitment means immense patience, courage to differ, and ability to undertake pain and suffering for one's dissenting voice. New ideas, any good historian of science would tell us, are not accepted easily. Instead, ridicule, social isolation and even boycott from the peer group await the destiny of revolutionary scientists who dare to differ, and question the massive dogmatism of 'normal'/routinized science. To quote Thomas Kuhn:

> Copernicianism made few converts for almost a century after Copernicus' death. Newton's work was not generally accepted, particularly on the continent, for more than half a century after the *Principa* appeared....The difficulties of conversion have often been noted by scientists themselves. Darwin, in a particularly perceptive passage at the end of his *Origin of Species* wrote: 'Although I am fully convinced of the truth of the views given in this volume, I by no means expect to convince experienced naturalists whose minds are stocked with a multitude of facts all viewed, during a long course of years, from a point of view directly opposite to mine. But I look with confidence to the future—to young and rising naturalists who will be able to view both sides of the question with impartiality. And Max Plank, surveying his own career in his *Scientific Autobiography* sadly remarked that 'a new scientific truth does not triumph by convincing its opponents and making them see the light, but rather because its opponents eventually die, and a new generation grows up that is familiar with it (Kuhn 1970:150-51).

In other words, the point I am trying to plead for is that it is not correct to tell children as if scientific theories were eternal and ahistorical, and scientists just happened to discover these truths, and got instant recognition. Instead, while studying science, let children learn that science, like any other activity, is also about intense contestation and struggle over priorities, and it could not have evolved without the dedication and commitment of some of its leading adherents. This is to humanize the very narrative of scientific progress. While teaching Newton or Galileo or Einstein, if a science teacher also shares their biographies with young children, science would indeed acquire a new meaning. It would not look like a technical/puzzle-solving exercise taking place in isolation; instead, it would emerge as our own story: a story of struggle and contestation, yet a story of courage, conviction and dedication.

Science as openness

There is yet another important value—a sense of humility—

that science education ought to radiate. How often in the name of science one becomes arrogant (yes, this arrogance emerges out of the dogmatism of 'certainty'), and begins to see only verifications and confirmations of one's theory all around, and, therefore, devalues and degrades all alternative possibilities. But then, an inherent principle of science education, it has to be realized, is a realization that nothing is stable like a rock; even a celebrated scientific theory, as Karl Popper showed with a remarkably brilliant insight, is like a 'conjecture' that may be falsified and replaced by a new one (Popper 1972). In other words, a sense of humility—or willingness to accept the ethos of refutability—is what gives a new meaning to science. I would further add that this humility is important because the domain of the unknown is so vast that it is simply impossible to remain indifferent to other voices and possibilities. Paul Feyerabend might have gone to an extreme while pleading for an 'anarchist' theory of knowledge (Feyerabend 1975); but the central message he conveyed remains significant. We all are fellow travellers, and even if one's path appears to be the most successful and celebrated one, one should not deny the experience of all those who have travelled through different trajectories. I would, therefore, like every student of science to recall what Feyerabend argued so convincingly:

> Non-scientific ideologies, practices, theories, traditions can become powerful rivals and can reveal major shortcomings of science if only they are given a fair chance to compete. It is the task of the institutions of a free society to give them such a fair chance. The excellence of science, however, can be asserted only after numerous comparisons with alternative points of view (Feyerabend 1987:103).

Science as sensitivity

In fact, this sense of humility becomes complete only when there is a high degree of *sensitivity* to life, to nature, and to the wonderful creation we see all around. Because science, if not taught properly, can also make one utterly insensitive to the beauty of creation. The reason is that science often demystifies, and, to use Max Weber's language, this 'disenchantment' may well become a beginning of alienation from the wonder/ mystery of nature. For example, when a child is told—and told very forcefully with all factual evidence—that the sun is just a source of energy; rains are there merely because of the water cycle; and the rainbow can be explained only in terms of refraction, it may cause some sort of violence to the child's imagination, her urge to talk to nature, and experience wonder and mystery in the sun, in the rains, and in the rainbow. This is not to promote prejudices and superstitions. This is only to suggest that science, even though immensely important, is just one way of understanding nature; it has no right to devalue other experiences which are possibly more intuitive, imaginative and intimate. Take, for instance, the way a young learner of science is generally told about the sun:

> The sun is a huge ball of swirling gas. It is mostly hydrogen gas and helium gas. Gold, iron, and all the other elements that are found on earth are also present in the sun, but the sun's heat keeps them in the form of gases. These gases press incredibly hard toward the centre of the sun. This pressure causes tremendous heat. The heat and pressure make the atoms in the sun's centre combine, or fuse. This fusion of atoms causes a huge nuclear reaction like the explosion of millions of hydrogen bombs, giving off great amounts of heat and light (Brand 1985:13-14).

Yes, this is an important fact. Had I been a physics teacher I would have definitely communicated this discovery to a young learner; but at the same time, I could have certainly shared a piece of poetry by William Blake:

> *My mother taught me underneath a tree*
> *And sitting down before the heat of day,*
> *She took me on her lap and kissed me,*
> *And pointing to the east began to say,*
> *Look at the rising sun: there God does live*
> *And gives his light, and gives his heat away.*
> *And flowers and trees and beasts and men receive*
> *Comfort in morning, joy in the noon day*
>
> (Quoted in Bloom and Trilling 1973:71)

Because, as I feel, science need not negate the intensity of poetic imagination. In fact, poetry can make us realize the limits of scientific analysis. Even John Passmore—a strong proponent of science—feels that science should leave us free 'to contemplate nature with enjoyment, with sensuous pleasure'; the fact that the woman we love is a cloud of electrons should not stop us 'conversing with her as soon as we start reading theoretical physics' (Passmore 1978:64)!

This sensitivity cannot, however, be taken for granted. Essentially, we need an innovative pedagogy to assert this point time and again because science with its cult of objectivity, value-neutrality and dispassionate analysis has a tendency to reduce everything into an object if experimentation. No wonder, from massive technological violence against nature to genetic engineering: complex moral/ethical issues are involved. Take, for instance, the danger of increased harmful radiation from the sun as a result of our depleting the ozone layer of the upper atmosphere through the use of fluorocarbons as propellants in aerosol cannisters, or the precipitation of acid rain which can upset the balance of lakes and rivers, and is thought to result from the output of sulphur into the atmosphere. Or, see the way we encourage young learners to dissect a living animal like a frog or a rat, and make them utterly insensitive to the moral question: how do animals respond to the violence inflicted on them in the course of study by humans? Krishna Kumar is right in arguing that 'if concern for the environment and the sensitivity to nature that it implies are to be reflected in school science as a whole, the curriculum of science will have to be designed differently' (Kumar 1996: 53). One cannot hide these ethical issues in the name of objectivity. Science should not free itself from compassion, from an experience of beauty and wonder. Yes, while studying the Newtonian theory of colours, let a student of science not forget that there is indeed divinity in the changing colour of the sky during the sunset; and to get thrilled by it is by no means a 'fall' from the world of reason, but it is essentially an experience of profound human sensitivity. Or, knowing the anatomy of human body should not prevent one from appreciating the wonder of goddess Durga's ten hands! After all, it should not be forgotten, as Robert Merton pointed out in his significant work on *Puritanism, Pietism and Science*, that for many scientists, 'the study of nature enables a fuller appreciation of His works and thus leads us to admire the Power, Wisdom and Goodness of God manifested in his Creation' (Merton 1972:628). Learning science with compassion and sensitivity, and with openness to alternative modes of engagement with life and nature would rescue it from its mere 'instrumental' use: the way these days it gets appropriated by the techno-corporate elite for mindless growth, consumption and profit.

II
THE MUSIC OF MATHEMATICS

Let us now come to mathematics—yet another branch of school knowledge. Its appeal, it is argued, lies in its ability to make one develop logical/analytical reasoning. Imagine a child calculating the value of the third angle in a triangle, when the values of the other two angles are given. Yes, she is developing deductive reasoning. Or, for that matter, when a child calculates the average speed of a train from the given values of distance and time, she learns a very important lesson of reasoning: how to draw a logical conclusion from the two given premises. Not solely that. Mathematics, one is told, demands constant practice, and its exercises—if done repeatedly—help the learner to evolve the power of speed and efficiency, and thereby think rationally and quickly. And we all realize that this faculty does have immense significance in life—not only in the domain of calculation, measurement and quantification, but also in diverse situations, say, when one is required to make an appropriate choice after evaluating a set of complex options; when one learns the grammar of a language; when one plays chess; or when one drives in an unknown city, and reaches the destination after penetrating into the city map. It is in this sense that one can say that mathematics is not just about arithmetic, trigonometry, geometry and algebra. Mathematics is essentially about logic and reasoning—about an important component of human life.

But then, why is it that mathematics is often feared, and, as experiences suggest, repels innumerable young learners? A possible reason is that we often erect a wall between reason and emotion, thinking and feeling, science and narrative, and theory and practice. No wonder, mathematical reasoning, for a child, tends to become abstract, decontextualized and disembodied—separated from the rhythm of life, its specificities and its experiences. It is being projected as an abstract science of numbers—a set of algebraic equations and geometrical theorems. How frequently our children are bombarded with such abstraction: '*The co-ordinates of the centroid of a triangle are (1,3) and two of its vertices are (-7,6) and (8,5). Find the vertex of the triangle*'. Or, '*Find the value of k for which the system of equations 3x+y=1; (2k-1)x +(k-1)y=(2k+1) has no solution*'. With such bombardment begins what is widely known as mathematics phobia. It becomes exceedingly difficult for the child to relate to mathematics, or to make sense of its relationship with the kind of life one leads, or sees around. Instead, the coldness of mathematics—its abstraction and impersonality—begins to cause terror. Although there are children who survive, it is difficult for many to live with this experience of violence—the way dispassionate reasoning disturbs the tender mind of the child: the mind that loves narratives relating to local contexts, and wishes to experience the rhythm of connectedness. A school child did enlighten me when she narrated the entire experience so vividly:

> *I sometimes wonder why numbers have always frightened us, why every maths class seemed like a sea we had to swim through, why every maths class came as a nightmare.... Probably there is a fault in the way it is taught. Numbers just remain part of complicated sums in the book, and never a part of life.*[4]

Yes, a child is a keen observer. She sees a lot of geometrical shapes all around—on the floor of the room she studies, on the chairs, tables, cups and glasses she uses everyday. She sees the monetary exchange and associated calculation when her papa/mummy buys milk and vegetable. And she experiences the actual use of fractions/decimal when milk, food, biscuits and apples are shared and distributed. These experiences—which are embodied and rooted in concrete life-situations—are seldom taken care of while mathematics is being taught to the school child. It is really sad that we forget that reason too needs to operate itself in a context, and it is always mediated through concrete life-experiences. It is, therefore, not surprising that more often than not, mathematics textbooks look terribly boring; utterly devoid of the sweetness of social relationships and aesthetic beauty.

See the irony. A child is asked to measure the area of a trapezium which she has not possibly handled, but has seen only as a two-dimensional picture in the textbook. But seldom is she asked to measure the length and breadth of her own room. Or, seldom is she inspired to interact with the tailor, and actually measure the length of the piece of cloth she buys for school uniform. It is sad that more often than not, school mathematics fails to encourage the child to respect the *experiential reality*, and evolve a way of seeing: say, experiencing the joy of discovering *parallel lines* while moving through a railway track, or measuring the volume of the football as a *sphere* that she plays with. Mathematics, as a result, appears to be merely an exercise in intellectual cognition—not something that is dear to the child: touching, feeling, doing and experiencing. If it is so severely dissociated from the music of life, how can it arouse the child's interest?

Not solely that. This abstract reasoning is often privileged over other important faculties of learning—say, literary imagination, creative intuition and emotive expressiveness. It is not surprising. Because modernity—particularly, the ethos of the techno-corporate world—is centred on this reasoning: its ability to quantify, measure, calculate, rationalize and evolve what is now known as an *objective* solution to a well- defined, tangible and non ambiguous problem. Numbers are everywhere: from death rate to fertility rate, from cricket statistics to stock exchange. Numbers are indeed sacrosanct in modern times. As a matter of fact, mathematics is seen to imply precision and objectivity—all the 'virtues' of modernity! Without mathematics, it is thought, there is no reasoning, and without reasoning there is no entry into the techno-corporate world. Physics is mathematics; commerce is mathematics; economics is mathematics; and even sociology, as some of its technicians would argue, is incomplete without mathematics. Mathematics is, therefore, all-pervasive. That is why, there is excessive pressure on the child to excel in mathematics. One cannot feel relaxed with it. It is being done with perpetual fear and insecurity. At times, this phobia causes disinterestedness; the child begins to lose interest in the culture of learning itself. Because the message she receives from school teachers, from parents, and from all sorts of public examinations is that once mathematics betrays her, she is doomed—bound to be declared as a 'failure': a defeated soul with 'feminine' anarchy and ambiguity, and not fit for hard techno-economic sciences.It is, therefore, not at all uncommon that if one fine morning we open up the newspaper, and find a report like this:

> Tension for examination has claimed another victim, this time a 17-year old student of a government school. Poonam's suicide note points to stress as she was 'very weak' in mathematics. A day before her Class XII Board examinations were to begin, the body of Poonam was found hanging from the ceiling fan of a room at her Mansarovar Park residence in north-east Delhi. Poonam was a student of commerce stream in Shahadra Girls' Government Senior Secondary School, and mathematics was her optional subject. According to her suicide note, the police said, she particularly dreaded mathematics.[5]

One meaningful way of removing such terrible fear, I guess, is to make it nearer to the world the child lives in. It is absolutely important to make the child realize that mathematics need not necessarily be something distant and remote—a science of soulless numbers. It is essentially a language—yes, a special language—to make sense of the world she experiences every day. Mathematics can be felt as yet another narrative to represent the world. It is in this sense that mathematics can be used meaningfully and creatively to sensitize the child. It can be as colourful as history or literature.

Some would object to this proposition. They might argue that mathematics is 'objective' and 'value-neutral' without having politico-ethical or subjective implications. But the fact is that it is a myth. Beneath its value-neutrality lies the story of legitimating what I would regard as a mercantile component of social reality. Let us take *arithmetic*—a major component of school mathematics. How often the child is told—particularly, when, she learns about *fraction, percentage, compound interest, profit* and *loss*—about the mercantile world, and its instrumental rationality. Take any text you want, and you would discover with utter dismay that it is full of exercises that reduce a human relationship into a mere contract between the buyer and the seller:

> A merchant purchases a wrist watch for Rs. 450, and fixes its list price in such a way that after allowing a discount of 10%, he earns a profit of 20%. Find the list price of the wrist watch.
>
> A trader marks his goods at 45% above the cost price, and gives a discount of 20%. What gain per cent does he have?
>
> A sum of money doubles itself at a compound interest in 15 years. In how many years will it become eight times?

Yes, as these exercises (and they reveal the general pattern, not the exception) suggest, the world that a standardized mathematics text portrays is essentially about buying and selling, and profit and loss. Where is then the much-talked about 'value- neutrality'? The fact is that mathematics is legitimating the ethos of the market. That is why, the challenge is to strive for an alternative pedagogic milieu in which mathematics can be used in generating a humane/reflexive consciousness that can have an appeal to the tender mind of the child. None is arguing that the world of trade and commerce does not exist. Yes, it does exist, and the child sees the market all around: in the *Mother Dairy* counter from where she buys ice cream or in the bookshop from where she buys her mathematics textbook. It is definitely important to learn about it. But then, the child's world is not just the world of the market. It is also a world filled with friendship, neighbourhood ties, games and sports; it is a world of joy, love, excitement, and the ethos of giving, sharing and taking. Mathematics, let it be realized, would do a great job, if it can also help the child to make sense of this world—much more meaningfully and intelligently. For example, the child can be encouraged to see the use of fraction while sharing her tiffin with a friend, or while observing that her mother does not mind sharing the fruits which have grown in their own garden with the next-door neighbour. Likewise, the child can learn the application of percentage not simply in the marketplace but also in the other exciting domains of human life—in the stories of distribution and sharing in everyday world.

> 'Do you have some extra milk? This evening I didn't get it in the Mother Dairy counter'—Mrs. Basu asked Mrs. Tiwari. Mrs. Tiwari had 4 lt of milk, and she offered 1.5 lt to Mrs. Basu. What per cent of milk did Mrs. Tiwari give to Mrs. Basu?
>
> What is the least number of bananas you need to buy so that you can give 1/2 to your sister, 1/3 to your friend, and 1/6 to your brother without cutting any of these bananas into pieces?.
>
> In a small library there are 50 mathematics books, 70 science books, 80 literature books, and 60 social science books. Mrs. Mary has decided to donate 40 new literature books to the library. After her donation, what fraction of library books would consist of social science?

These alternative exercises—no less intellectually challenging and stimulating—tell a different story; one is not just a buyer and a seller; one is also a friend, a neighbour, a comrade! If mathematics becomes sensitive to this story which every child loves to experience, it can indeed emerge as yet another language—no less beautiful than poetry and music. It would gain the aesthetic sensibility that would remove much of its abstraction and remoteness. It would enable the child to live with it, and eventually undertake a journey from the concrete to the abstract. I am aware that there are some who would argue that not every component of school mathematics can be translated into tangible social realities and experiences. Mathematics, it would be argued, is also about abstraction, and children must develop the capacity for abstract reasoning. Yes, I see a point. As children enter higher classes, and are invited to the domain of *calculus, matrix* and *set theory,* they need to evolve a taste for abstract logic. However, abstraction has to begin from lived experiences. My own interaction with school children (even when they are at Class X) suggests how difficult it is for them to visualize the specificity of a situation, and then solve a problem like this: '*As observed from the top of a light house 100 m high above sea level, the angle of depression of a ship, sailing directly towards it, changes from 30° to 45°. Determine the distance travelled by the ship during the period of observation*'. There are children who have not seen the sea closely. Nor have they got an opportunity to see the movement of a ship. The entire exercise, as a result, looked terribly bookish; and even those who solve it, as a perceptive mathematics teacher would concede, do so by memorizing the formula with all its stages. That is why, my central argument is that unless a taste is developed for experiential mathematics, most of them would develop terrible fear, and fail to appreciate higher mathematics.

As a matter of fact, *learning through doing,* as Mohandas Karamchand Gandhi tried to articulate in his own way, is an important pedagogic device; it helps the learner to experience the spirit of connectedness between thinking and practice, and cognition and work. Mathematics, in order to be meaningful to the child—particularly at junior classes—does indeed require this integral approach. It is really unfortunate that today if you ask a child about the height of the room in which she studies, she may have to think twice to give even an approximate estimate. Or, for that matter, a school-going child may not have the kind of efficiency that we often witness amongst 'illiterate' street hawkers while engaging in everyday calculation. The reason is that seldom do schools teach mathematics as a meaningful engagement with the lived world. However, for a clear understanding as well as joy of learning, this creative engagement—or, operationalization of mathematical concepts in the domain of everyday life—becomes absolutely necessary. Possibly, an engagement of this kind leads to critical consciousness. I have often wondered how a child would respond if she were given a challenge of this kind:

> A bottle of Pepsi costs Rs. 10. And the same amount of lemon water costs Rs. 2. By what percent does Pepsi cost more than lemon water?

Can an exercise of this kind be reduced into just a kind of 'efficiency' in calculation? Or, does it also make the child think why Pepsi costs more, even when lemon water is such a healthy drink? I am not suggesting that a mathematics teacher has to be a political economist. Nor am I suggesting that a school child is capable of comprehending the business logic of transnational economic corporations. What I, however, wish to plead for is that once mathematics is related to lived realities, the entire experience of learning begins to alter. And from just a 'skill' in calculation it becomes an *awakening*. I would, therefore, suggest: let a child be asked to measure the space that her bookshelf occupies, and compare it with the space that electronic devices like television and washing machine occupy in her house. Let a child be asked to do a project on the average consumption of milk in, say, families of different income groups. Or, let a child be inspired to learn statistics through the classification of students at her own school in different age groups. If illuminating projects of this kind become the norm rather than the exception, three important functions are likely to be served:(a) it would arouse interest in mathematics because the child would discover something that makes sense to her life, and the world she lives in; (b) it would help the child to activate her energy—body as well as mind—in the process of learning; and (c) it would save school mathematics from being reduced into a mere intellectual exercise—a sort of puzzle-solving activity. Instead, it would emerge as a life-affirming, relational, aesthetically rich and child-friendly endeavour. And it is likely to succeed in reducing what is known as 'mathematics phobia'. Furthermore, mathematics too would begin to sing the music of life: its finer moments of togetherness, solidarity and above all, sensitivity to social issues.

III
THE WONDER OF HISTORY

Like science and mathematics, history too is an important component of school knowledge. Yes, today when I have grown up and passed through diverse experiences of life, I can appreciate the significance of history. Without history, I realize,

I cannot make sense of my biography, or think of my future. It enables me to locate myself in time and space, and appreciate that the language I speak, the religion I adhere to, the tools I use, and the ideologies I celebrate have evolved and emerged out of a long and continual process. In other words, I realize what Fernand Braudel would have said: no social phenomenon can be understood adequately 'if it does not attach itself to the movement of history, to the resounding dialectic which runs from the past to the present, and even to the future (Braudel 1980: 80). History is indeed alive, vibrant and immensely illuminating. Yet, as I look back, and think of my schooldays, I see yet another projection of history as a body of knowledge—full of discrete facts, dates of war, revolutions and treaties, and names of kings, empires and monuments; and everything, as we were told, ought to be memorized for its own sake. There was no intellectual stimulation, no inner realization, and no analytical framework to make sense of these bundles of facts and events. That was the tragedy.

Things are, however, changing. These days a highly sophisticated and elevated debate on historiography, let us hope, would make educators and teachers sensitive to the depth of history. It is indeed wonderful that today when I look at the recent NCERT textbook in history for Class XII, I find an altogether different projection of history. Ancient India, for example, acquires a new meaning when one is asked to reflect on different *themes* (rather than memorizing discrete facts)—say, 'bricks, beads and bones' to make sense of the Harappan civilization; 'kinship, caste and class' to know the nature of early societies; and 'thinkers, believers and buildings' to comprehend the dynamics of culture. Possibly we are realizing that history is not just about grand/spectacular episodes like the rise and fall of empires; history is also about people, their modes of existence, and their struggles and aspirations. And this evolution of social history, it is said, can also be understood through new inventions and discoveries, and through conflict of different politico-economic and cultural forces, and resultant social movements. To put it otherwise, history can be made nearer to people's life-experiences. Moreover, history, let it be emphasized, is not a soulless documentation of dead facts. History, wrote Marc Bloch, has its 'aesthetic pleasures', because 'the spectacle of human activity which forms its particular object is, more than any other, designed to seduce the imagination—above all when, thanks to its remoteness in time or space, it is adorned with the subtle enchantment of the unfamiliar' (Bloch 1954: 8). Even though history as an organized body of knowledge is capable of satisfying the intellect, its 'poetic quality', adds Bloch, is its privilege—its ability to arouse a sense of wonder.

Does this sensitivity get reflected in school history? Is it possible to teach history in a refreshingly different manner? Even though, as I have just mentioned, there is innovation in the recent NCERT venture, everything depends on the kind of pedagogic purpose with which the teacher comes to the classroom, and engages in the transaction of knowledge. It is in this context that I wish to mention that there are four possibilities which are absolutely important for an alternative mode of teaching/learning history:

History as a sense of humility

History, to begin with, has a powerful ethico-moral component. The more we study history the more we realize how important it is to grow humble. Isn't it a fact that many of us—particularly, in modern times—tend to think that we are far superior to our ancestors because we possess what they were deprived of: scientific reasoning, technological development and liberal democracy? Or, as Bloch stated brilliantly, 'the man of the age of electricity and of the airplane feels himself far removed from his ancestors. With less wisdom he has been disposed to conclude that they have ceased to influence him' (Ibid: 36). This epistemological/cultural supremacy—or this sense of a radical departure from our past—may prevent us from seeing and appreciating how we actually evolved, progressed and arrived at the present stage. History in a way gives us the much-needed sense of continuity. This is indeed a great lesson—how not to absolutize ourselves, and instead, see our limited roles in the long trajectory of human evolution. I believe that this sense of wonder and awe has to be felt by every young learner while studying history. Imagine, for instance, a child being told—and told meaningfully—about our *cave architecture* at Elephanta, Ajanta and Elora. This is bound to arouse a sense of humility. True, modern architecture has immense achievements; yet how wonderful it is to think of those finest pieces of architecture constructed in the distant past! Or, as I have often felt, while discussing the *Vedic age* (a period which may have many discontents), if a teacher of history recites a couple of Vedic hymns, it is bound to have a profound impact on the tender mind of the child. Think of the following hymns:

> *This light is come, amid all lights the fairest; born is the brilliant, far-extending brightness*
> *Night, sent away for Savitar's uprising, hath yielded up a birthplace for the Morning* (RV. I: 113.1).

> *This light, the best of lights, supreme, all-conquering, winner of riches, is exalted with high laud.*
> *All-lighting, radiant, mighty as the Sun to see, he spreadeth wide unfailing victory and strength* (RV. X:170.3)

Yes, as one is encouraged to appreciate the very poetic beauty of these hymns, one begins to realize that literature is not just what we notice today with its Nobel and Booker Prize winners; in fact, the poetic sensibility that characterized our ancestors in such distant past makes us humble. This sense of humility I am referring to does not, however, mean that history is about romanticizing, sanctifying and glorifying our past. A lesson of history is also about our past follies and wrong deeds—say, about racism, casteism, slavery and feudalism. Nor does an engagement with history mean getting excessively nostalgic, and thereby belittling our modern achievements. The only thing that I am talking about is that in the past too there were people like us—no less vital, imaginative and creative. A child ought to learn this lesson of history. This is the beginning of humility, an experience of continuity, and a feeling of connectedness. Even today, despite my adulthood and possible cynicism, whenever I visit the National Museum I experience a sense of wonder. For example, as I look at the achievements of the Harappan civilization: its artefacts, its sculpture, its wonderful creations like the *dancing girl* or the *head priest*, a sacred feeling of reverence, humility and beauty envelops my consciousnesses. That is history. It enters my soul. It gives me a sense of continuity. Jawaharlal Nehru's 'discovery' of India, I believe, gave us this taste of wonder. True, Nehru was immensely modern—known for his 'scientific temper', his romance with techno-scientific development, and his faith in the new age. Yet, his historical sensitivity generated a sense of humility. Despite his criticality, he could look at the past with great respect:

> We can never forget the ideas that have moved our race, the dreams of the Indian people through the ages, the wisdom of the ancients, the buoyant energy and love of life and nature of our forefathers, their spirit of curiosity and mental adventure, the daring of their thought, their splendid achievements in literature, art and culture, their love of truth, beauty and freedom, the basic values they set up (Nehru: 1984: 509).

Let children experience this wonder. History, for them, ought to be enchanted.

History as a continual flow of time

Another possibility of history is that it can rescue the past from being degenerated into a reified category—a dead material to be kept in the museum or the archives. Instead, an engagement with the past—a creative mode of pedagogy would convince us—gives a new meaning to our present. Or, to put it otherwise, our contemporary needs and concerns often shape our ways of seeing our past. This linkage between the past and the present, or experiencing time as a continual flow is what, I believe, a child ought to be encouraged to understand. I remember we were once telling little children a fascinating story of Ashoka while doing a workshop with them: how the mighty emperor got himself involved in the Kalinga war, caused and experienced massive bloodshed and devastation, and eventually realized the futility of war, and became committed to the Buddhist doctrine of peace and love. While we were doing this workshop, there was yet another devastating war taking place: the war in which the mighty United States attacked Afghanistan and Iraq.

No wonder, we asked the children: 'do you feel that President George W. Bush could do what Ashoka did?' They were too young. They did not have the answer. But then, in their own ways they could possibly make sense of what we were hinting at: recurrence of war in history, and also our longing for those extraordinary moments of realization when we feel the futility of war. No wonder, at the time of Afghan and Iraq war, Ashoka, for the children, became immensely alive, vibrant and contemporary—possibly a reference point linking our present concerns with the past, and thereby enchanting it. As a matter of fact, we live in a society that experiences a series of paradoxes: secular ideal and communal politics, egalitarian aspirations and caste hierarchies, and religious pluralism and exclusivist cultural nationalism. These contradictory and conflicting trends can also be seen in our past. But then, if we want—which, I believe, we should—an egalitarian/inclusive society, we can also see its roots in our heritage, in our past. Bloch was absolutely right in showing that 'it is always by borrowing from our daily experiences and by shading them, where necessary with new tints that we derive the elements which help us to restore the past (Bloch 1954: 44). It is in this context that Kabir, for instance, should not remain merely a footnote or a paragraph in a school history text; instead, he should emerge as a living figure inspiring us to overcome all sorts of exclusion and limitedness:

> *O SERVANT, where dost thou seek Me?*
> *Lo! I am beside thee.*
> *I am neither in temple nor in mosque:*
> *I am neither in Kaaba nor in Kailash:*
> *Neither am I in rites and ceremonies, nor in*
> *Yoga and renunciation*
> *If thou art a true seeker, thou shalt at once*
> *see Me: thou shalt meet Me in a moment*
> *of time*
> *Kabir says, 'O Sadhu! God is the breath of all breath'*[6]

Yes, if we interpret our history through the present discourse of cultural syncretism or secular humanism, Kabir becomes immensely relevant. As Bloch would have argued, 'the knowledge of the present bears even more immediately upon the understanding of the past' (Ibid: 45). Indeed, from Kabir to Gandhi—there was a continuity. It is this wonderful experience of the fusion of the past and the present that gives a new meaning to history. And children must be encouraged to have a pulse of it.

History as illuminating narratives

Anyone who has interacted with children knows that they love beautiful narratives; they love the way great characters unfold their stories. This fascination with life and its extraordinary moments is something which, I believe, history as a discipline—particularly, when communicated to children—must cultivate. I am not saying that children should be encouraged to indulge in hero-worshipping. Nor am I arguing that history should be used as a tool for valorizing and sanctifying select characters. I have something else in mind. Let, to the child, history manifest itself through human stories: stories of anxiety, failure, suffering, love, hope and rebellion. Because

> behind the features of landscape, behind tools or machinery, behind what appear to be the most formalized written documents, and behind institutions, which seem almost entirely detached from their founders, there are men, and it is men that history seeks to grasp....The good historian is like the giant of the fairly tale. He knows that wherever he catches the scent of human flesh, there his quarry lies (Ibid: 26).

And let a meaningful engagement with these stories arouse the child's faith in life. For example, a school student in India studies quite a lot about the history of the freedom struggle. But this history is not just about a chronicle of events, movements, pacts and treaties. What is equally fascinating is the historic context in which illuminating characters unfolded their possibilities. Take the case of Mohandas Karamchand Gandhi. The task is not just to tell the child about the three mass movements (Non-Cooperation, Civil Disobedience and Quit India) that Gandhi led. There was also a man called Mohandas—exactly like us, with follies and mistakes, and hopes and aspirations. His story of evolution would indeed give a new meaning to history, and fascinate the child. Imagine a dialogic teacher of history asking a child to read the following stories from Gandhi's *Autobiography*:

> My friend once took me to a brothel. He sent me in with necessary instructions. It was all prearranged. The bill had already been paid. ...I sat near the woman on her bed, but I was tongue-tied. She naturally lost patience with me, and showed me the door, with abuses and insults. I then felt as though my manhood had been injured, and wished to sink into the ground for shame. But I have ever since given thanks to God for having saved me. I can recall four similar incidents in my life, and in most of them my good fortune, rather than any effect on my part, saved me (Gandhi 1976: 16-17).
>
> ....The other theft was committed when I was fifteen. In this case I stole a bit of gold out of my meat-eating brother's armlet. This brother had run into a debt of about twenty-five rupees. He had on his arm an armlet of solid gold. It was not difficult to clip a bit out of it....But this became more than I could bear. I resolved never to steal again. I also made up my mind to confess it to my father. But I did not dare to speak....I decided at last to write out the confession, to submit it to my father, and ask his forgiveness. I wrote it on a slip of paper and handed it to him myself....He read it through, and pearl-drops trickled down his cheeks, wetting the paper. For a moment he closed his eyes in thought and then tore up the note. He had sat up to read it. He again lay down. I also cried. I could see my father's agony. If I were a painter I could draw a picture of the whole scene today. It is still so vivid in my mind. Those pearl-drops of love cleansed my heart, and washed my sin away (Ibid: 19).

The train reached Maritzburg, the capital of Natal, at about 9 p.m. Beddings used to be provided at this station. A railway servant came and asked me if I wanted one. 'No', said I, 'I have one with me'. He went away. But a passenger came next, and looked me up and down. He saw that I was a 'coloured' man. This disturbed him. Out he went and came in again with one or two officials. They all kept quiet, when another official came to me and said, 'Come along, you must go to the van compartment'. 'But I have a first class ticket', said I. 'That

> doesn't matter', rejoined the other. 'I tell you, you must go to the van compartment'. 'I tell you, I was permitted to travel in this compartment at Durban, and I insist on going on it'. 'No, you won't', said the official, 'You must leave this compartment, or else I shall have to call a police constable to push you out'. 'Yes, you may. I refuse to get out voluntarily'. The constable came. He took me by the hand and pushed me out. My luggage was also taken out... . It was winter, and winter in the higher regions of South Africa is severely cold. Maritzburg being at a high altitude, the cold was extremely bitter. I sat in the waiting room and shivered.... I began to think of my duty. Should I fight for my rights or go back to India, or should I go on to Pretoria without minding the insults, and return to India after finishing the case? It would be cowardice to run back to India without fulfilling my obligation. The hardship to which I was subjected was superficial—only a symptom of the deep disease of colour prejudice. I should try, if possible, to root out the disease and suffer hardships in the process (Ibid : 82).

This trajectory—Gandhi's fall, his emotional vulnerability, his shame and guilt, and yet his inner strength and immense commitment—does convey a message to the child: none of us is born as a genius; we make mistakes, we fail, we suffer; yet, we stand up, acquire courage, and make our presence felt. This is to realize that it is not just Gandhi, but we all have potential—the capacity to love, revolt and think of others; and revolutions take place only when collectively we unfold this potential. It is in this sense that, for a child, history can indeed act like an epic—a source of meaningful human stories. And I would argue that we have no right to deprive the child of this charm of history. Amidst the load of information and factual details, these illuminating narratives which are dear to the child's mind should not be forgotten.

History as democratization of consciousness

Finally, history can also fight a sense of fatalism that often confronts us. We tend to think that history is being made only by the select elite, and we are simply passive spectators. A penetrating look at history does, however, reveal a different story. Yes, people—ordinary people—fought, suffered, struggled and transformed their society. Take, for instance, the historic illustration of the freedom struggle. Our children should not be given the impression that one Mahatma Gandhi, one Subhas Chandra Bose, or one Bhagat Singh gave us the much-desired freedom from colonialism. As a matter of fact, these grand histories could be sustained only through innumerable local histories: there were many unknown Gandhis and Bhagat Singhs who struggled and suffered and did wonders. Ranjit Guha made this point abundantly clear when he argued that

> parallel to the domain of elite politics there existed throughout the colonial period another domain of Indian politics in which the principal actors were not the dominant groups...but the subaltern classes and groups constituting the mass of the labouring population and the intermediate strata in town and country—that is, the people (Guha 1994:4).

The pedagogic challenge is that these histories—these local narratives, or, to use Guha's language, the 'autonomous domain' of the people—too ought to be communicated to children. I have often wondered how fascinating it would be for a teacher of history to tell them the story of Birsa Munda: a tribal hero from Chhotanagpur who, much before the arrival of Mahatma Gandhi, Subhas Chandra Bose and Bhagat Singh, inspired his community to fight a heroic battle against the British rule in order to protect their land rights. True, as Sumit Sarkar has argued convincingly, 'seeking a conscious all-India nationalist in Birsa is obviously futile because his vision could not have embraced anything broader than a heroic defence of his tribal homeland against all intruders' (Sarkar 1983: 48). Yet, what cannot be denied is that these very histories which speak of extraordinary stories of ordinary people ought to become an integral component of children's imagination. This is to realize that people matter, and they are capable of making a difference. It is in this sense that history, if taught with great care and sensitivity, can democratize and decolonize our consciousness.

As a matter of fact, in our times this pedagogic challenge has acquired added relevance. 'Why is it that India has always lagged behind? Why is it that there is nothing heroic in India?

And why is it that all good things—modernity, scientific revolution, liberal democracy, material prosperity—had their origin in the West?' These were indeed complex questions a school student once asked me. Possibly as educators we could not convince them that even though the great Enlightenment did not take place in India in the eighteenth century, we were not living in a dark age; and there were remarkable achievements—from music to trade, from philosophy to literature—made by our ancestors. We could not convince them that the West's material success was not necessarily because of their inherent merit; it was primarily related to colonialism—its doctrine of plunder and profit. And now as the ideology of global capitalism further reinforces the duality of 'development' vs. 'underdevelopment', it becomes exceedingly difficult to convince them. Herein lies the relevance of history. The aim of history, I repeat, is not to romanticize our past. But history is also an awareness: a critical imagination that can make these children feel that we can not overcome our shortcomings if we continue to stigmatize ourselves; instead, we move ahead only when we see our strength and potential. What else is decolonization of consciousness?

IV
THE REFLEXIVITY OF SOCIAL SCIENCE

This sense of history, I guess, helps children to understand what is often being taught in the name of 'civics'. It is in this context that I wish to refer to the foundations of our Constitution: a major component of school social science knowledge—particularly, at middle and higher stages of schooling. Yes, for a child, it is important to be aware of our Constitution because it is an embodiment of our collective aspirations. History teaches us that the Constitution emerged out of a prolonged struggle for decolonization, and subsequently our quest for a new society. In a way, the ideals of the freedom struggle were articulated in the Constitution. I have always believed that learning about the Constitution should not be seen as a mechanical process: just memorizing our fundamental rights, directive principles, and rules/articles governing the electoral process and formation of legislative bodies—the way one accumulates discrete pieces of information for participating in a quiz contest! Instead, it is essentially about developing a new sensitivity to appreciate and realize our shared humanity through mutual respect and collective participation. In fact, all these fundamental rights and directive principles, it should not be forgotten, emerged out of these egalitarian ideals. My freedom of expression, my right not to be get discriminated against, and exploited, and the ethical responsibility of the state to take care of my well-being define my humanity, and reaffirm my dignity as a person. And without this self-esteem we cannot create a good society. I therefore, believe that concepts like 'rights', 'socialism' 'secularism' and 'welfare state' need to be communicated in a manner that makes the child realize the beauty of this ongoing quest for a more humane world. It is indeed nice to see a school text communicating the concept of 'individual freedom' in a manner which is both ethically sensitive and analytically mature:

> The first point to note about the Constitution is its commitment to individual freedom. This commitment did not emerge miraculously out of calm deliberations around a table. Rather, it was the product of continuous intellectual and political activity of well over a century. As early as the beginning of the nineteenth century, Rammohan Roy protested against the curtailment of the freedom of the press by the British colonial state. Roy suggested that a state responsive to the needs of individuals must provide them the means by which their needs are communicated. Therefore, the state must permit unlimited liberty of publication. Likewise, Indians continued to demand free press throughout the British rule. It is not surprising therefore that freedom of expression is an integral part of the Indian Constitution. So is the freedom from arbitrary arrest. After all, the infamous Rowlatt Act, which the national movement opposed vehemently, sought to deny this basic freedom.[7]

This pedagogic sensitivity—which I regard as the reflexivity of social science—can also make the child see the prevailing gap between the ideal and the real. True, the Preamble of our

Constitution narrated our collective aspirations for a just society. But then, the reality we confront is by no means free from violence, inequality and exploitation. It is difficult to hide this domain of darkness from the child. Newspapers, television visuals, and even whispers and adult discourses in the family make the child see and feel the reality of conflict all around: be it communal tension or caste prejudice or sexual violence. Furthermore, a child has keen eyes; she often sees that children of her own age group, instead of going to school, are working in a tea shop, in a factory, or even in her own household as a domestic help; and even if she is growing up in a privileged colony in a metropolis, it is difficult not to see the striking contrasts: luxurious/fortified apartments vs. ghettoized slums; beauty queens in fashion shows vs. children of construction workers begging in the street. I do realize that an awareness of such heightened conflict, particularly for a tender mind, is a painful process. Imagine the way a school child from Delhi has expressed her deep anguish:

Another era has passed.
I can already hear
Those wine glasses clink,
False hearty laughter
And dull speeches on past developments...
Something in me awakens and asks "Oh really?"

* * *

This world speaks of equality,
Then why a wall between the affluent and the destitute?
Why a barricade between the flair and the dusky?
Why a hedge between the high class and the low?
Why a food fest for the fortunate gluttons,
While not even a crumb for some?
Why a fashion fury—meaning full fledged wastage,
While not even rags for some?
"But wait. This is just the end of an era,
We'll see to it in future..."[8]

Seeing through conflict and cooperation

Yet, as I wish to argue, a sense of conflict has its pedagogic significance. It is through an awareness of the prevailing social conflict that we realize what we really are: how power operates in a society, and how it divides and fragments. We also understand how society progresses through conflict—through a sustained struggle by people to eradicate the roots of inequality, and create the foundations of a just society. Moreover, it is also an awareness of belonging to a struggling group, be it a caste or a class or an ethnic association, that arouses an intense zeal for striving for an egalitarian society. In other words, conflict is not necessarily a 'law and order' problem. An awareness of conflict and its meaningful political articulation can force history to move towards progress. I am not suggesting that school students—particularly, the younger ones—are necessarily mature enough to comprehend what social scientists regard as 'conflict theories' emanating from Marxism and its dialectical logic. Anyone who has interacted with children knows how wrong and violent it is to bombard their minds with our complex theories and discourses. That is why, their tenderness, sensitivity and cognitive development ought to be taken into account for any meaningful pedagogic intervention into the domain of conflict and violence in society. I would rather argue that the real challenge is how to communicate the reality of conflict with a high degree of sensitivity and empathy so that it does not make them pessimistic or cynical. Instead, let them evolve a critical/constructive consciousness, engage in a penetrating dialogue with the parents, teachers and adults, and get inspired to appreciate and implement yet another component of social existence: the story of solidarity and cooperation.

In fact, an awareness of conflict becomes truly meaningful when one also understands the dynamics of social cooperation. Because in the ultimate analysis it is the spirit of cooperation and togetherness which we strive for. Even those who speak of conflict are dreaming of and fighting for a society filled with the ethos of unity and solidarity. Marxism strives for a future communist society free from alienation, fragmentation and exploitation. Feminists celebrate a society that sees beyond the patriarchal duality and violence. Possibly the message is that even though we are conflict-ridden beings, we are capable of living together with a sense of cooperation. And this faith can emerge only when we see that everyday reality, even at its worst form, is not just about violence, injustice and exploitation. It is also about love, collective concern and a spirit of working together. As solitary individuals, Emile Durkheim taught us, we cannot live; we exist because we exist together, and constitute a network of social relationships that bind us. Or, as Gandhi showed through his unique method of *satyagraha,* even when we resist and protest against injustice, we can have a deeper realization of human unity. Social science, it should not be forgotten, should also enable the child to comprehend the significance of this process. It is in this context that I wish to refer to the twin examples of *collectivities*—family and nation—which school social science texts often deal with. Yes, a family is the most intimate experience of cooperation a child can relate to. How incomplete one is without the love and care of one's parents, grandparents and siblings. Realizing this, as any social science teacher would admit, is like realizing the limits to egotism, and understanding the first lesson of social cooperation. This linkage between the individual and other fellow beings gets further developed as the child moves beyond the family. She can be encouraged to see equally important stories of social solidarity in a neighbourhood, at her own school, or in the larger society. In this sense learning social science is also like learning the value of social cooperation: how to think of others, and evolve shared norms and values. Only then would collectivities, far from looking like abstract and distant entities, would emerge as intimate zones of togetherness. Or, to use the language of formal social science, it would enable the young learner to appreciate the significance of a vibrant *civil society*: a set of intermediary institutions that exist between the family and the state.

In this context we can think of a complex notion like 'nation'. Every sensitive teacher would admit that it is not easy to make the child understand the meaning of 'nation', or for that matter, the meaning of being an 'Indian.' Because even though a child can identify with more tangible collectivities like a family, a club or a school, it is not easy to conceptualize a nation which we adults often regard as an 'imagined community'. Moreover, there are strikingly visible differences emanating from the diversity of languages, religions, dietary practices and cultural beliefs. Is there, then, a 'nation: a collectivity called India with shared memories and histories? A lesson of history is that how, despite innumerable differences, we lived together, interacted with one another, got inspired by some common literature, epics and ideals; how we fought and suffered together in the process of decolonization; and how we got our political freedom, and pledged to consolidate a sovereign nation-state. Or, for that matter, geography taught us about the distinctiveness of our territory: how its rivers and mountains, its climate and crops, its natural resources and modes of transport and communication have entered deep inside our collective imagination. Likewise, social science, if taught creatively, can tell the child how some of our everyday experiences transcend the boundaries of family, caste and religion: say, when the Indian Railways take us from Jammu to Kanyakumari; when people from all over the country exercise their voting rights, and send their representatives to Parliament; and when we constitute public institutions and universities which remain open to all. These experiences of transcending limiting identities and boundaries can make one understand a broader reality called India. With such awakening social science can indeed enable the child to have a sense of 'citizenship'. One is not just a Bengali or a Tamil; a Brahmin or Dalit; one is also an Indian; and this identity of 'Indianness' emerges because we have chosen to live together under one polity called the nation-state How important it is for social science to make the child realize that conflict is not the only story of our existence; we can cooperate and live together.

The story of cooperation and unification does by no means suggest that school social science should be reduced into a statist construct: a device for consolidating the 'ideological apparatus the state'[9]. In fact, as I wish to emphasize once again, the reality of asymmetrical power relations and resultant conflict do not escape the attention of even a tender school-going child. It is not altogether difficult for a child to see that even an 'intimate' zone of the family is a site of conflict—say, between the patriarchal father and the subjugated mother, or between the pampered male child and the neglected female child. True, the child may not be able to articulate it in terms of what we are otherwise used to: sophisticated feminist theories. Nevertheless, the child experiences the reality of power and conflict, and this awareness must be acknowledged in the process of teaching/ learning. As a school text of sociology[10] questions the one-sided emphasis on cooperation and altruism in the family, and begins to articulate the story of substantial conflict of interests, and thereby the need for resistance, we realize that things are changing. An intervention of this kind does indeed encourage the child to feel the need for a more humane/egalitarian/ gender-sensitive family. Likewise, even though 'Indianness' is a grand ideal, the fact remains that there are people who do not enjoy what political theorists regard as a central characteristic of citizenship: 'full and equal membership'. Tribals, oppressed people from marginalized castes and communities, and ethnic minorities often feel a sense of marginalization and stigmatization. This leads to a disturbing question: for whom is the nation? Yes, children, as they grow up and come to higher classes, ought to be encouraged to raise this question: not to deconstruct 'Indianness', but to get inspired to create a space for a more inclusive citizenship. A school text of political science, it seems, is hinting at this possibility when it writes:

> The Constitution adopted an essentially democratic and inclusive notion of citizenship.... However, even such inclusive provisions have given rise to struggles and controversies. The women's movement, the dalit movement, or struggles of people displaced by development projects, represent only a few of the struggles waged by people who feel that they are being denied full rights of citizenship. The experience of India indicates that democratic citizenship in any country is a project, an ideal to work towards. New issues are constantly being raised as societies change and new demands are made by groups who feel they are being marginalized. In a democratic state these demands have to be negotiated[11].

To put it otherwise, conflict is real, but cooperation is a possibility. Or, the spirit of cooperation is our potential that has not yet fully manifested itself. From conflict to cooperation, from violence to peace, from fragmentation to solidarity—this is a journey. And social science should make our children believe in the beauty of undertaking such a journey. In fact, this entire exercise of learning through life-affirming optimism as well as critical sensibility is an exceedingly subtle task that can be done only through sympathy, excellent pedagogic principles, and continual dialogue with the child. Because the idea is to evolve and nurture a reflexive mind that thinks, feels and cares; a mind that is critical, not cynical; a mind that protests, yet loves.

V
LITERARY IMAGINATION AND AESTHETIC SENSIBILITY

Learning language is yet another significant component of school experience. Indeed, language with its oral and written articulations is something that distinguishes the human species. Language enables us to describe and define the world, and communicate with others. In this sense language empowers us. Yes, as a mode of communication it is something special about our social existence. And in modern times—particularly, after the arrival of the printing press—written words have acquired added significance. Thoughts, ideas and information get recorded, codified, and disseminated quickly. Indeed, 'written words', as Scott-James stated brilliantly, 'contain all the letters, and are used by all the writers' (Scott-James 1956: 337). No wonder, no domain of mental energy, be it religion or philosophy, politics or physics, policy or morality can escape the influence of written words. It is through written words, as Scott-James emphasized, mankind becomes 'conscious of itself in every way' (Ibid: 337). Education in our times, therefore, demands the continual cultivation of the skill of reading, writing and communicating. It is like having one's own language to represent the world one experiences.

But then, learning language, it should be remembered, is not just about learning its grammar and other technicalities.

Language is essentially a mode of communication through which we narrate our stories, and understand the stories told by others. This interest in human stories seems to be eternal. And anyone who has lived with children knows how curious they are to read and listen to these stories. It is this natural curiosity which, I believe, has to be cultivated while teaching language to children. Possibly a school teacher needs to remind herself time and again that there is a distinction between a dictionary (which is either accurate or inaccurate) and a literary narrative whose excellence lies in its beauty, not in its technical accuracy. A child's taste for such beauty should by no means get disturbed because of our excessive preoccupation with the accuracy of grammar which, strangely enough, continues to be the dominant practice of language teaching. In other words, learning language is like getting increasingly inclined to what I wish to regard as *literary sensibility*. In fact, this literary sensibility has a profound ethical component. It creates a bond between the writer and the reader, between the story teller and the listener. It is like generating a community that induces its participants to listen to one another: their love and hope, and pain and suffering. An extremely valuable thing that literature can do for us is to reveal 'the existence of a kind of common basis of feeling' because it is only through literature that we come to realize that 'others have had the same feeling as ourselves and have been able to understand them, and bring them to light' (Coombers 1963: 89). This awakening is not instrumental and calculative. It softens the mind and touches the heart. It enables us to see beyond the mundane, and make us truly attentive to life. To quote Scott-James once again:

> It rescues us from the inattentiveness and obtuseness of the so-called real life, from that diminished state of half-awareness—a matter of sleeping and waking, knives and forks, bus fares and gossip—in which we lose the vividness of experience and miss the characteristics of the life that passes and passes.... It clutches at anything which promises some permanence among what is always fleeting. It loves *rhythm* and *pattern* because theirs is a recurrence which may go on for ever and ever (Scott-James 1956: 344).

Not just great stories, novels, poems and literary pieces, but even letters—when written with care and concern—have such immense power; they fulfil the human need to see beyond oneself and embrace others. I am referring to letters because schoolchildren in their language classes are often encouraged to write diverse forms of letter: letter to a friend, letter to one's parent, letter to a government official, or letter to a newspaper editor. At times, this entire exercise is done in a ruthlessly standardized form (merely for functional needs) which tends to deprive the learner of experiencing the very beauty of a letter. And particularly in our times when the culture of instant communication through electronic mail and SMS messages has further devalued the literary significance of letters, it is rather important for a language teacher to take her job seriously. I have often felt like sharing with children Nehru's letters to his daughter. Take, for instance, a beautiful letter Nehru wrote from the prison to his daughter:

> What a mountain of letters I have written! And what a lot of good *swadeshi* ink I have spread out on *swadeshi* paper. Was it worth while, I wonder? Will all this paper and ink convey any message to you that will interest you? You will say, yes, of course, for you will feel that any other answer might hurt me, and you are too partial to me to take such a risk. But whether you care for them or not, you cannot grudge me the joy of having written them, day after day, during these two long years. It was winter when I came. Winter gave place to our brief spring, slain all too soon by the summer heat; and then, when the ground was parched and dry and men and beasts panted for breath, came the monsoon, with its beautiful supply of fresh and cool rain water. Autumn followed, and the sky was wonderfully clear and blue and the afternoons were pleasant. The year's cycle was over, and again it began: winter and spring and summer and the rainy season. I have sat here, writing to you and thinking of you, and watched the seasons go by, and listened to the pitpat of the rain on my barrack roof... (Nehru 1989: 949).

What a letter! It has its rhythm: deep sensitivity to life and nature. It emerges out of an urge to communicate the intensity of feeling. It touches the soul. This letter is, however, just an illustration. Even if ordinary mortals like us look at our own biographies, we are bound to discover the significance of great letters written by us, or written to us. These letters symbolize the depth of human feeling: our longing for a communion, and our urge to invite the intimate ones to our inner world. We, however, see an altogether different story emerging from our classrooms. 'Draft a suitable **notice** for your school notice board informing students about a seven day camp at Nainital'. Or, 'Your house is available on rent in a posh colony for the diplomatic core. Stating the details including the expected rent, draft an advertisement for a national daily'. Or, 'You are Sandeep Verma of 59 Sena Road, Bandra, Mumbai who sees an advertisement in *The Indian Express* and decides to apply for the job of a Sales Executive. Write an application with your resume to the Personal Manager, U.K. Publications, Mumbai'. As school students are bombarded with the exercises of this kind, I realize how functional needs have become overwhelmingly powerful in these pragmatic times. Even though one cannot deny their importance, we have to realize that learning language is not just about acquiring the technical skill of writing formal applications or notices or newspaper reports; it is primarily about acquiring a profound aesthetic/ literary/humane sensitivity.

Not solely that. It is through literary sensibility that one learns yet another faculty of cognition—creative/intuitive imagination. Mathematical/logical reasoning, we all know, has an important role to play. Yet, reason is by no means the only faculty of cognition. We also make sense of the world through intuition and creativity. And this understanding is by no means unreal. Instead, we penetrate beneath the apparent reality, and begin to see what lies hidden. Great stories, fictions and novels take us to that domain; the depth of a character a writer portrays becomes nearer to us, and we also take an inward journey. How often through literary texts we rediscover ourselves. It is in this sense that great literature transcends the boundaries of time and space. Let me recall an illuminating conversation I once initiated with a school student:

'Do you like literature?'

'Not necessarily the way it is taught at school'.

'You mean to say that you do not like literature'.

'No, I am not saying that. I like it in my own way'.

'Can you elaborate?'

'I haven't read much'.

'Still?'

'I like only those pieces I can relate to'.

'Examples?'

'I have read Hemingway's Old Man and the Sea and Austen's Pride and Prejudice'.

'But they lived in a different era, in a different society. How can you relate to them?'

'They must have communicated universal human feelings. That's why, I could relate'.[12]

How important it is for children to experience the intense bond with literature, and get a pulse of what life is all about: its depth, its pain, its strivings. And how wonderful it would have been had schools given due space to language teachers to generate such sensitivity. As I look through the NCERT textbook in English for Class XII, a piece of Pablo Neruda's beautiful poem 'Keeping Quiet' strikes my mind. But then, I can feel that the very joy of reading such a poem—a poem that talks about the necessity of quiet introspection and creating a feeling of mutual understanding among human beings—would be sacrificed because, after everything said and done, Neruda, almost like a frog in the biology lab, would be fragmented into pieces, and the child would be asked to read an extract like this: *Perhaps the Earth can teach us/ As when everything seems dead/ And later proves to be alive/ Now I will count up to twelve/ And you keep quiet and I will go*; and then answer a set of typical questions: (a) What does the Earth teach us? (b) Why does the poem count up to twelve? (c) What will keeping quiet help us achieve? That is the way poetry gets murdered in the classroom.

I am referring to poetry because its rhythmic beauty fascinates children. Furthermore, with poetry, every good language teacher must have realized, begins an important lesson: how to see what, because of the burden of everydayness, we often miss—say, the way a romantic poet would have revealed 'eternity' in a tiny blue flower, or a Vedic poet would have discovered Indra's promise (of bringing rain) in the lightning in a clouded sky! In other words, it is to see beyond the routinized, and enter the realm of metaphor and aesthetic imagination. I love to recall our experience of a workshop with school children, particularly when we shared with them a piece of poetry written by William Wordsworth way back in 1802:

My heart leaps up when I behold
A rainbow in the sky:
So was it when my life began;
So is it now I am a man;
So be it when I shall grow old,
Or let me die!
The child is father of the Man;
And I could wish my days to be
Bound each to each by natural piety.

Yes, the children, even though situated in the twenty-first century urban milieu, could feel the charm of the poetry. Their hearts did indeed leap up; they could experience the wonder of nature. Poetry releases this creative energy. And children, let schools realize, ought to be inspired to enter this poetic domain for experiencing wonder, mystery, love, beauty and harmony. As Coleridge would have argued, poetry bridges the gulf—unbridgeable by the intellect—between perception and understanding. The power which the poet exercises in revealing 'the beautiful and permanent forms of nature' is the 'shaping spirit of imagination', a unifying creative faculty—'the beautiful and beauty-making power' (Quoted in Scott-James 1956: 220). When should schools realize that it is precisely this sensitivity that is the strength of literature?

Furthermore, this sensitivity, I wish to add at this juncture, also manifests itself in many other forms of cultural creation—say, music, dance and painting to which children, I guess, are intrinsically inclined. Through his experimentation in the domain of education, Rabindranath Tagore wanted to teach us this basic truth. However, the irony of our present system of education is that these 'softer' domains continue to be regarded as 'extra curricular', and thereby often devalued in comparison with the 'major' curricular and 'hard' options like mathematics, science and geography. I would also argue that even the cultivation of the physical body has a role to play in this aesthetic education. In fact, physical education need not necessarily be seen as just physical education; it can be elevated to a finer aesthetic sensibility. Walking, trekking and gardening have their own aesthetics; yoga and other related exercises have their deep understanding of the aesthetics of human body—the unity of the physical and the spiritual; and even football and cricket can prove to be immensely artistic. It is, however, unfortunate that games and sports—major components of physical education at our schools—have become terribly narcissistic, competitive and tension-ridden with an urge to cultivate only the 'killer instinct'. Moreover, in the age of television-mediated culture, children get the message that the 'killer instinct' sells because there is absolute marketization and commodification of sports. Not solely that. Even gender stereotypes and hierarchies are reproduced. Masculinity with its physical aggression and competitiveness is expected to manifest itself in power games that boys play. Likewise, the fitness of girls is often seen to be an exercise in cultivating the 'feminine' beauty that must charm men. Possibly this orientation cannot be separated from the recent proliferation of 'beauty industry' in which the human body becomes a site of surveillance; it must be continually observed, kept under strict dietary regime, and shaped/ modulated/marked/trained/decorated for fulfilling the needs of the market, and its gender ideologies. Can schools with an emancipatory pedagogy make an effort to alter this perception of human body, and create a new possibility which sees beyond the market and its gender stereotypes, as well as what Michel Foucault would have regarded as disciplinary devices for cultivating 'docile' bodies? This requires the ability to see the unity of the body and the spirit. In other words, games and sports need not be seen as just a professional training for cultivating social Darwinism—for declaring 'winner' and 'loser'; instead, these activities can be performed in an altogether different manner: for relaxing the nerves and the muscles; for generating a sense of joy and abundance in a domain that is not crudely utilitarian; for evolving a spirit of ecstasy and togetherness; and for retaining the thrill without losing one's calm—the way the *Bhagavadgita* would imagine an active doer engaged in worldly activities, yet having a sense of detachment. It is only in this sense that a hockey player running with the stick and performing wonders, or a gymnast expressing the waves, rhythms and flexibility of the human body generates great moments of inspiration which, I believe, are bound to tempt an artist to make excellent portraits. Only then can poetry and literature, music and dance, yoga and football merge. Can children be deprived of this realm of fusion?

VI
CONSTRAINTS AND POSSIBILITIES

The critical pedagogy and its implicit purpose of creative and life-affirming learning, one may argue, often get defeated because of real obstacles that confront the prevalent system of education in India. There are primarily three hurdles—(a) excessive dominance of textbooks; (b) examination-centric learning; and (c) hierarchy of knowledges and professions—we need to reflect on, and eventually overcome.

Seeing beyond textbooks

To begin with, let us reflect on textbooks which play an excessively important role in the transaction of school knowledge. This is constraining for many reasons. First, seldom do these texts arouse joy in learning. Because they carry a heavy load of information (and information, it is sad, is generally equated with knowledge) that further denaturalizes the entire experience of learning. And textbooks—often written by scholars burdened with their own knowledge, and by no means organically linked with the experiential domain of children—become more important than the world itself: the world children live in, and relate to. The dominance of textbooks confines them to the four walls of the classroom. Seldom do they get an opportunity to see and experience diverse sources of knowledge in the larger world: poetry in nature, in lived relationships; geography and history in the art of travelling—moving through varied places and landscapes; and geometry in architecture and urban designing. Instead, everything has to be learned (or memorized?) from the prescribed text. It enslaves the learner as well as the teacher. Not solely that. Barring exceptions,[13] there is not much scope for involving the child in the text. Seldom does one find dialogic and creative space in these texts. Instead, the language is alienating and impersonal. No meaningful relationship between the child and the text is allowed to develop. I feel tempted to give an example from the NCERT textbook of psychology for Class XI. While introducing the 'experimental method', the text gave the following example:

> Two American psychologists, Bibb Latane and John Darley, conducted a study in 1970. In order to participate in this study the students of Columbia University arrived individually at a laboratory. They were given the impression that they would be interviewed on a certain topic. Each student was sent to a waiting room to complete a preliminary questionnaire. Some of them found two other people already seated in the room, while others sat down alone. Soon after the students had started working on the questionnaire, smoke began filling the room through a wall vent. The smoke could hardly be ignored; within four minutes the room contained enough smoke to interfere with vision and breathing. Latane and Darley were primarily interested in knowing how frequently students simply got up and left the room to report the emergency. Most (75 per cent) of the students who were waiting alone reported the smoke, but those reporting in groups were far less. Groups consisting of three naïve students reported it only 38 per cent of the time. When the students waited with two other confederates, who were instructed before hand by the researches to do nothing, only 10 per cent students reported smoke.[14]

What a style of writing! Does anyone make sense of it? Hard facts bombard the mind of the learner; there is taboo on subjectivity; the self of the writer or the reader is completely withdrawn from the text; and truth is projected as a fact existing out there which one can cognize only intellectually, and that too with extreme difficulty. It should not be forgotten that it is only in Class XI that a student, for the first time, is invited to the formal discipline of psychology. At this stage an attempt should be made to arouse the learner's interest with everyday examples she can identify with. But the language of the text is so impersonal and distant that there seems to be no possibility of a meaningful and engaged learning. As psychology becomes a 'science', it fails to make an appeal to the inner world of the child. The alienation from the text is not limited to only one discipline. It seems to be all-pervasive. See the agony of school children:

> It is boring. It is presented in a very dull manner. It doesn't appeal to me.
>
> Not very interesting. At times, I am not even convinced about what a particular textbook of a particular discipline has to offer me.
>
> Though they adhere to the syllabus given, they should also change with the changing times and be more relevant to the current scenario.[15]

Second, textbooks as 'legitimate' sources and carriers of knowledge tend to constrain the teacher. In fact, the autonomy of the teacher, her creativity, and her right to experiment do not get realized when she is asked to rely primarily on the prescribed text— its chapters, its illustrations, and even the set of questions it carriers at the end of each section. Creativity demands reflexivity and the spirit of innovation. The beauty of teaching as a vocation or the charisma of a teacher, I have always believed, lies in the process of perpetual exploration. Ironically, however, the prevalent textbook-centric culture reduces the entire process of learning into a dull, predictable, routinized exercise, and diminishes significantly the role of the teacher. She becomes merely a mediator between the text and the child. It is really sad that not many policy makers and educationists in India have given a serious thought to this problem. Take, for instance, the ongoing debate on the ideological character of textbooks—say, whether a history textbook is sufficiently 'secular', or inclined towards the worldview of the dominant religious community.

This debate in which both the leftists and the rightists engage remains, however, silent on the central issue we are posing: the creative autonomy of the teacher. Instead, it is assumed that only if appropriate textbooks (for the leftists, these should be written by 'secular' scholars, and for the rightists, these should be authored by 'cultural nationalists') are available, the educational system would be salvaged!

I am insisting on something qualitatively different. No text, irrespective of its ideology, should be allowed to play a hegemonic role in the transaction of knowledge. Let the teacher and the child explore the world together, break pre-given structures, raise new questions, and find diverse sources of knowledge. I have often imagined myself in the role of a school-teacher. I would not like any textbook—even if written by the most celebrated scholar—to restrain me in the classroom. For instance, if I engage with children, and explore India's composite culture, why should it prevent me from doing what the text does not otherwise prescribe—say, reciting Kabir's *doha* in the classroom, or talking about Bollywood—the way Javed Akhtar writes the script, R.D. Burman composes the music, Amitabh Bachchan plays the lead role, and people in Chennai celebrate the film! These are possibilities spread all over society, culture and everyday life which every creative teacher would like to explore. Limiting or constraining a teacher, and instructing her to remain confined only to fixed structures, chapters, pages and questions would deny the very joy of teaching.

I do admit that we need some guidelines, or what can be regarded as a broad cognitive map to explore the world. And select books—if written with great care and imagination—would definitely help the teacher as well as the student for evolving a framework, a vantage point. But then, these texts need to be seen merely as a catalyst: something that just opens up the window, and then makes it possible for the teacher as well as the learner to explore with freedom and joy. How wonderful it would have been had our children been encouraged to see beyond prescribed texts, and read, say, Bhagat Singh's diary while studying the revolutionary trend in the freedom struggle; or interact with rural peasants to know more about climate, crops, harvesting and social geography. Yes, seeing books as enabling, not constraining means immense creativity on the part of the teacher. This requires a new social environment that, instead of focusing merely on external qualifications, invites truly creative minds—those who love children, do not hesitate to experiment, and have the talent and passion for transaction and communication of ideas, experiences and information—to the vocation of teaching, nurtures them, and gives them what they need(infrastructure, learning material, financial security and above all, social recognition) for retaining their zeal and enthusiasm. In other words, this is to restore agency to the vocation of teaching. Likewise, this is to have faith in the child's active participation in the quest for knowledge. This is to attach special importance to what I would regard as *learning through doing*.

No to examinations and regimentation

This, however, becomes exceedingly difficult because of the prevalent practice of examinations, and evaluation of students. Examinations, as it is argued by the enthusiastic adherents of the system, work efficiently, and make it possible to evaluate a child's cognitive development. This is similar to what Talcott Parsons would have regarded as the process of selecting people for manpower allocation (Parsons 1968). For example, through examinations, as Parsons said, schools convey a clear message: those who do well at the secondary level would join colleges for higher learning, and those who don't would be required to join the labour force! In other words, examinations, it is argued, would keep the child perpetually alert, and force her to try to perform better. Yet, if we see beyond their apparent functions and think deeply, we do realize that exams, because of their very nature, lead to excessive psychic stress, put children under terrible pressure; and it becomes simply impossible for them to open up, unfold their potential with ease and comfort, and learn with a sense of joy and freedom. Instead, exams, it seems, are designed to keep children under the disciplinary gaze and its techniques of surveillance. Exams, Michel Foucault was quite perceptive in arguing, are like 'ceremonies of power' through which schools observe, monitor, document and hierarchize children (Foucault 1982: 184–94). No wonder, a schooled mind grows up with perpetual fear, anxiety and insecurity. It is, therefore, not surprising that such a culture leads to a parallel industry—an industry dominated by all sorts of experts, psychiatrists and counsellors—that advises children 'how to eat and sleep well, and get some exercise to reduce the exam tension'. See, for instance, how a nutrition consultant wrote her column in a national daily before the board exams:

> I find myself in a peculiar situation these days. My son is preparing for his school board exams and I must confess that I am prone to some anxiety on account of his diet. Friends and colleagues in the same boat are keen to know my prescription.... First and foremost, it should be remembered that memory or recall is a complex process that is closely linked to good blood circulation and nerve health. So it is important to eat the right kind of fats as this is extremely crucial in maintaining nerve health.... The ideal fat/oil for children would be one with adequate ratio of Omega 3 fatty acids. Try to use oil derived from mustard seeds, rice bran, soybean, olives, canola or sesame seeds. It will be worthwhile to slip in some nuts and seeds—watermelon and sunflower or walnuts—into salads and cereals. All this will enhance the desirable fat content of their diets.[16]

In a way, her column shows what exams have done to our consciousness. As we get more and more wounded, the 'expertized' advice begins to proliferate. It further intensifies the tension. The fear of exams has indeed entered deep into our collective consciousness. Not solely that. Exams also lead to a sense of terrible competitiveness; everybody becomes one's possible opponent: a lesson that children learn the moment they join nursery classes. This is possibly the reason why such a practice, as it is feared, might erect a huge wall between 'success' and 'failure', 'achievers' and 'losers', and eventually lead to the 'totalitarianism of the elite' (Singha 1984: 64–73).

Moreover, exams, I would argue, promote a cult of quantification which devalues a child's specificity, qualitative distinctiveness and uniqueness. Exams are supposedly 'neutral', having a uniform/universal scale through which a child is evaluated, quantified and hierarchized. But then, it should not be forgotten that each child has her own distinctive experience of learning. One may be inclined to abstract theorization; another may feel comfortable with concrete life-experiences. One may have a high degree of oral articulation; another may have a good writing skill. One may be oriented to mathematical reasoning, and another to poetic sensibility. All these differences are, however, eliminated, and at the day of judgment—the day of final examination at the end of the year—a set of questions manufactured by anonymous experts is distributed amongst all, and children, irrespective of their specificities and socio-cultural locations, are ranked through a uniform scale. This is not neutrality. Instead, as Bourdieu (1977) has taught us, this is nothing but violence (or symbolic violence): violence against the uniqueness of the learner, violence against the very rhythm of learning and its varied and rich experience. Under these circumstances, what emerges is the fetish of ninety per cent. If you do not have it, you are nothing, you are a failure!

I have yet another serious objection to exam-centric learning. What it claims—i.e., evaluating a child's critical/creative thinking—is seldom achieved. Because exams, any careful observer would agree, are terribly mechanical, and as a result, one's success rests primarily on a strategy: the practice of mindless drilling, memorizing and evolving some sort of ruthless efficiency in answering all the questions in the allotted time and space. This symbolizes a training in regimentation rather than an inclination to exploratory learning. Take, for instance, the pattern of questions in social science that the CBSE board generally formulates for Class X:

1. Why is Raja Rammohun Roy known as the father of Modern India?
2. Who built the Sanchi Stupa?
3. Write four points on W.C. Bonerjee.
4. What is human development index?
5. What is WTO? When and why was it set up?
6. Write a note on soil erosion.
7. Distinguish between natural and cultural resources.

This sample indicates that for a learner there is not much scope for creative articulation and critical thinking. Instead, what is required is instantaneity: the ability to provide a fixed and readymade answer (often learned through mass circulated 'guide' books). It constrains the learner, forces her to remain limited to 'four main points' or 'fifty words', and deprives her of thinking, imagining, reflecting, expressing and going deeper. Here I feel tempted to give an example. A student of Class XII from a reputed school in New Delhi once showed me the answer she wrote to a question her sociology teacher asked in the school examination. The specific question was about the concept of commodification. 'Commodification is a process through which', she wrote, 'even those things which are not meant to be bought and sold become victims of the market'. Furthermore, as she added, 'Indian spirituality in the form of Art of Living course, or an attractively packed video CD of Yoga postures is an example of commodification'. Here is an answer that shows the child's alert mind, and her ability to relate her sociological concept to the reality she experiences everyday. However, as she told me, her teacher was terribly disappointed because her answer was not in tune with the standard CBSE pattern. She was reminded that she must give examples from the prescribed text itself, and use the textual language. In other words, she got a strong message: criticality or sensitivity does not matter much; instead, what is important is rote learning. I do not blame the teacher. She too is a victim of the system that negates reflexivity, and forces children to follow the standardized path. Likewise, even if we look at mathematics—a paper which supposedly evaluates a child's 'intelligence'—we witness a similar process of mechanization. It does not judge how one thinks mathematically, and uses mathematics in everyday life. Instead, its sole purpose, it seems, is to evaluate how much psychic stress one can bear while solving a set of twenty-five problems in three hours—almost like a machine capable of providing a perfect response to a given stimulus! It is, therefore, not surprising that tutorial homes, coaching classes and guide books become an integral component of this pathology. The message is that one should confine oneself only to the set pattern, and not venture into any other creative quest. That is why, even the Chief Minister of Delhi, as a huge ad in a leading newspaper reveals, feels the need for reminding the students of the required exam strategy:

> All the 1.8 lakh students of schools run by the Government of Delhi appearing for standard 10 and 12 Board Exams are further informed that:
>
> - The Model test papers provided in the Question Bank which have been given to each and every student of standard 10 and 12 are based on the latest pattern and design of the CBSE question papers 2008.
> - the Pre-board examinations were also held on the same pattern and design.
> - hence all students of standard 10 and 12 are familiar with the pattern of the examination.[17]

Does it disturb a political sociologist? Yes, the state wants its future citizens to remain one-dimensional. Follow the pattern, do the predictable, and be successful! There is no reward for creative exploration. Does it indicate a hidden desire for fascist thinking?

My critique of exams, let me add, does by no means suggest that I am pleading for 'everything goes' sort of approach. Far from that. Children love challenges, and if faith is restored, and they are respected, they would come forward with remarkable activities. That is why, not exams in their present form, but a qualitatively different mode of evaluation is the need of the hour. Imagine a situation: a teacher asks her students to explore the world around them, and experience and make sense of *light and colour*. It is quite likely that someone would come forward with what physicists regard as the optical phenomenon; and someone might feel inspired to draw a painting of the changing colour of the sky during the sunset. These are all rich experiences of learning through which physics and aesthetics tend to merge. Or imagine yet another situation: a teacher of history asks her students (say, of Class X) to go through select chapters from the autobiographical accounts of Gandhi and Nehru, and write an essay on these two great minds: their similarities and differences.

And yes, exposures of this kind, every creative teacher would agree, would generate a far deeper understanding of physics, aesthetics and history than what happens through the prevalent practice, i.e. a quiz-centric examination pattern. For such experimentations, let me emphasize, we do not need elite schools. Every child is fond of new challenges. The only thing we need is our willingness to make a difference. Furthermore, the continual process of inviting them to new challenges would also lead to a refreshingly innovative mode of evaluation. It would resist quantification and comparison. It would not declare one's 'success' at the cost of someone else's 'failure'. Instead, it would act like a catalyst, and suggest diverse possibilities: how one can improve, evolve, understand one's uniqueness, and move towards the appropriate vocation. In a new pedagogic culture I would rather imagine a progress report like this:

> Possibly you need to have some more reading on the history of the freedom struggle. What is, however, interesting is that in the class you often used to imitate Mahatma Gandhi walking during the Dandi March, and amuse you friends and teachers. With the kind of theatrical skill you are gifted with, you may do well in aesthetic ventures like drama and cinema.

Or, think of yet another possible report:

> Yes, your writing skill—the way you explain the Newtonian law of gravitation, or different climatic zones in India—needs some improvement. However, what is striking is your spontaneity: the way you come forward whenever there is a dispute in the class. You try to resolve it; you seem to be friendly with all. Don't underestimate this strength of yours. Possibly you are destined to emerge as a social activist or a community leader.

How different these reports would be from what our children are otherwise used to: Mathematics-28; English-54; Social Science-65; Science-41; Hindi-37!

In other words, the very purpose of evaluation would begin to alter. One would leave the school neither with a sense of failure, nor with what popular media seek to inject into the minds of the 'achievers'—a celebrity syndrome; but with a humble feeling that none is useless, and everybody has possibilities which have to be further evolved, cultivated and protected.

Transcending homogenization of aspirations

Things are not easy. After all, we live in a society in which the hierarchy of knowledges and professions is often being reproduced through school education. In this hierarchy, professions relating to purely instrumental and techno-economic sciences occupy the top position, and all other options are regarded as 'soft'—not particularly lucrative and assuring, and hence supposed to be reserved for those who cannot make it to 'high status' courses. No wonder then, 'success' stories of schools, we often notice, are popularized through IIT/ Engineering/medical entrance test results: how many of their 'products' have achieved the much-desired goal! This entire exercise, I would argue, further legitimates and intensifies the culture of ruthless examinations—examinations for eliminating and processing people for select careers.

This excessive concentration on select careers and resultant societal and peer group pressure make it really difficult for young learners to look at themselves, and understand their own likes and dislikes. Nor do schools want, despite ritualistic references to career counselling and things of that sort, to create an environment conducive to the child's inner growth. Instead, it looks like a huge machine that breeds uniformity of aspirations (almost everybody believes that not to opt for science/ commerce is to accept one's failure, or if you happen to opt for humanities, you must take economics without which there is no salvation). Where is then the scope for finding one's vocation, or listening to one's inner calling? Or, for that matter, where is the scope for schools to make the child aware of her innate possibilities? Instead, when they enter Class XI, almost mechanically they are placed in the three streams: science, commerce and humanities which—anyone who is familiar with our school system knows—are ordered hierarchically. And it hurts the sensibilities of those who have chosen to opt for humanities, and undertake an altogether different trajectory:

> Yes, schools maintain the hierarchy, and our stream is used as a dumping ground by the teachers. Those who perform badly in the other streams are forced into ours[18].
>
> Science and Humanities students are not treated equally. All the weaker students are automatically put in the humanities stream. Moreover, facilities like the smart boards have been installed only for science and commerce students, and not for us. So yes, I believe that schools not only maintain this hierarchy but also encourage such thinking[19].

Under these circumstances, it becomes really difficult for a child to acquire self-confidence, and pursue her own path.

Can we do something to resist this ongoing loss of diversity and creativity? It is, of course, true that without a radical shift in social priorities (and these priorities have further been legitimated by the neo-liberal economy and its ethos of all-pervasive marketization), schools alone cannot do much. Yet, to move a step forward is to acquire the courage to think differently, and believe that alternatives are always desirable and also possible. In this context I would argue that it is necessary on our part—teachers, adults and parents—to encourage children to listen to the other stories: how people have fought and suffered, yet discovered their chosen paths and found a meaning in existence. Life is not necessarily a standardized/linear path to 'success': opt for science/ commerce, do your MBA, join a transnational corporation, get married, have children, and arouse the same ambition in their minds. Life has its turns, curves and rhythms that alter the very meaning of 'success' and 'failure'. What else is Franz Kafka's pain or Karl Marx's struggle, or Mohandas Karamchand Gandhi's assassination? Indeed, the challenge is to strive for one's *swadharma*, to pursue it, and to derive satisfaction in this process of continual exploration. A teacher, a dancer, an anthropologist, a farmer, a social activist, a geologist... there are innumerable life-histories amongst us which, if communicated meaningfully, have the power to make the child realize that creativity is not what one does, but how one does it, and it can be done with grace, and in silence. This is like regaining the ethical character of education, and defying the ruthlessness of the learning machine.

True, constraints are many. Without truly creative/ autonomous teachers; without relative autonomy of schools, and a fairly respectable teacher-taught ratio; and above all, without altering the very structure of the larger society, it may be argued, not much can be done. But then, we can overcome these constraints only if we visualize the future, and believe in the domain of possibilities. Moreover, despite constraints, we need to make a beginning, and move—even though with enormous difficulties—towards what every sane educationist strives for. And that is where lies the promise of a reflexive pedagogy.

NOTES

1. The positivist regime that emerged with the triumph of modern sciences was responsible for erecting a wall between science and metaphysics, fact and value, and reason and emotion. It also led to determinism and reductionism: an attempt to reduce the whole into some determining elements. As a result, holism, inter-connectedness and dialogue between science and religion became more and more difficult. However, in our times we are becoming increasingly sensitive to the discontents of the positivist perception of science. For further details, see Uberoi (2002).
2. Written response to my enquiry from a science student of Class XI of Bluebells School International, New Delhi.
3. Yet another written response to my enquiry from the same student.
4. Written response from yet another student of Class X of Bluebells School International, New Delhi.
5. From a report published in the New Delhi edition of *The Indian Express* (10.03.08).
6. This piece has been collected from an edited volume entitled *One Hundred Poems of Kabir* (Translated by Rabindranath Tagore). 1997. Delhi: Macmillan India Limited.
7. Quoted from the textbook of Political Science for Class XI: *Indian Constitution at Work*, 2006. NCERT: Delhi.
8. This poem, written by Divya Ranghanathan (XI-A) was published in *Blossoms* (p. 21)—the magazine of Bluebells School International.

9. According to Louis Althusser, education as an 'ideological apparatus' of the state spells out the 'rules of good behaviour' for the child's later economic role. For future wage-earners, it fosters the feeling of 'modesty, resignation and submissiveness'; for future capitalists, education instills a sense of 'cynicism, contempt, arrogance, self-importance, even smooth talk and cunning'. (Quoted in Blackledge and Hunt 1985:161)
10. I am referring to *Understanding Society* (Textbook for Class XI). 2006. Delhi: NCERT.
11. Quoted from *Political Theory* (Textbook for Class XI). 2006. Delhi: NCERT, (p. 92.)
12. Conversation with a former student of Mirambika School, New Delhi.
13. Yes, there are indeed exceptions. For example, recent NCERT textbooks of political science are refreshingly different. What strikes me is the spirit of dialogue in these texts. From R.K. Laxman's cartoons to examples from everyday life—these texts, I am sure, would succeed in engaging the child, and make her think and reflect. I have quoted from these books.
14. Quoted from *Psychology* (Textbook for Class XI). Delhi: NCERT (p. 29).
15. Quoted from my field diary based on my interaction with school students in New Delhi.
16. Quoted from Neealanjana Singh's column *Weight and Watch* published in the New Delhi edition of *The Indian Express* (23.02.08).
17. Quoted from an advertisement issued by Education Department, Government of NCT of Delhi, and published in the New Delhi edition of *The Indian Express* (01.03.08).
18. Written response to my enquiry from a student of Class XI of Bluebells School International.
19. Written response to my enquiry from yet another student of Class XI of Bluebells School International.

Chapter III

Beyond Instrumentality: Restoring the Spirit of Higher Education

The discussion in which we have engaged so far would remain incomplete without looking at the state of higher learning: the way universities generate and disseminate knowledges, raise new questions, and arouse human sensitivity. Even though as a learner one enters the university at a relatively mature stage, the process of socialization and internalization of ethical and cultural values, we all realize, does not stop. It would, therefore, not be wrong to say that there is a continuity in one's journey from school to university: one keeps learning, growing and evolving. In fact, it is not impossible to find people amongst us who would confess that university life, for them, has acted like a turning point, a catalyst making them rethink the world—its politics, values and ideals. Yes, we are familiar with its grand ideals, its humanism and its creative possibilities which have often been celebrated by great thinkers, educationists and visionaries. But then, a university, it has to be admitted, cannot exist as an insulated island; the flow of larger politico-economic forces, and socio-historical trends are bound to influence its ethos, its culture, and its orientation to knowledge and research. Not surprisingly, a university often becomes a site of contradictions: idealism vs. pragmatism; fundamental knowledge vs. market-driven instrumental research; and egalitarian humanism vs. elitist exclusion. Furthermore, in a country like ours, characterized by uneven development, scarcity of resources, and excessive pressure of ever-growing aspirants from diverse sections of society, our universities, barring exceptions, face yet another kind of crisis emanating from irrelevant curriculum, demotivated teachers and students, absence of a meaningful agenda of research and teaching, and above all, widespread campus violence. Under these circumstances, what can we do to restore the humanistic ideal of the university, and make it contribute to the cultural and ethical development of the individual and the larger society? In this chapter I wish to throw light on these complex issues, and further reflect on the possibilities of emancipatory education.

I
TRAJECTORY OF A VISION

To begin with, let me refer to the three ideals of the university which, I believe, are absolutely important for enabling it to contribute to the enrichment of human sensitivity and culture. First, what ought to characterize a university is its identity as a *whole* (not merely an aggregate of self-centred departments): the way it can become a confluence of diverse epistemologies and traditions of knowledge, and generate a truly dialogic space. Its promise, I would emphasize, is the cultivation of a mind characterized by perpetual alertness, a sense of humility, and willingness to learn and see beyond one's limited horizon. Would it be an exaggeration to say that the fate of democracy lies in such a dialogic consciousness? Living in a university, let us hope, is like fighting all sorts of limitedness and exclusion, and thereby celebrating the ethos of openness, plurality and democracy. Second, the symmetry of teaching and research should be seen as yet another significant ideal. Exploring new frontiers of knowledge, and sharing these exciting ideas with students; nurturing an intimate bond between the teacher and the taught; and contributing to the creation of a generation of thinkers, researchers, teachers and concerned citizens: these practices—if followed with zeal and enthusiasm—are capable of having a deep-rooted impact on the development of the mind—its calmness, its patience and endurance, and its commitment to fundamental questions relating to nature, life, culture and society. And third, the university as an embodiment of an alternative (or truly sane) culture filled with the principles of cosmopolitanism, gender equity and ecological sensitivity needs to be appreciated because only then is it possible to make an attempt to unite theory and practice, and arouse hope that Utopias are not dead. All these three ideals merge, and take us to the vision of a university that keeps its intellectual and ethico-moral quest alive, and refuses to measure itself purely in terms of the rationality of the market. It is important to situate these ideals in the context of the ongoing debate on the very purpose of a university—its higher objectives, its social functions, and its economic utility.

At this juncture, it would, therefore, not be wrong to recall John Henry Newman who indeed contributed immensely to the idea of a liberal university (Newman 1959). Newman was articulating his ideas in the mid nineteenth century. In fact, in the Discourses he gave in Dublin at the inception of the Catholic University in 1852, the idea of a liberal university became more obvious. Knowledge, he insisted, should be seen as an end in itself. 'That alone is liberal knowledge', argued Newman, 'which stands on its own pretensions, is independent of sequel, expects no complement, refuses to be informed (as it is called) by any end, or absorbed into any art, in order to present itself to our contemplation'. In our times it is, however, easy to dismiss him as an 'elitist' thinker who, as his opponents would allege, was not willing to give importance to man's practical needs, and instead, pleading for knowledge for its own sake, and even making a case of theology as a fundamental branch of knowledge in a university. It is also possible to argue that such an idea of liberal education would encourage only select aristocracy who alone can afford to forget 'utility' or practical needs of professional education (and its relationship with job, industry and market), and give their consent to what, for instance, Mark Pattison—a leading Oxford reformer in the nineteenth century—asserted:

> Universities are not to fit men for some special mode of gaining a livelihood; their object is not to teach law or divinity, banking or engineering, but to cultivate the mind and form the intelligence. A university should be in a possession of all science and all knowledge, but as science and knowledge, not as a money-bringing pursuit (Pattison 1876: 61-62).

We know that the idea of a liberal university that Newman, Pattison and their disciples were pleading for was not accepted by all. As society was changing because of a combination of science, free trade and democracy, hard questions were being asked, and the answers they evoked were radically to alter the idea of a university. In England itself an effort was made to persuade the universities to establish the links with professional training. For example, Lyon Playfair—a great entrepreneur and propagandist of science—differed significantly from the Oxbridge liberal tradition, and argued without any ambiguity: 'Unless our universities go with the stream, by fitting themselves to the changed requirements of modern society, need they be astonished if society soon gets accustomed to look upon them as venerable moments of a past age '(Playfair 1889: 377). Indeed, with this declaration of social need and utility, as Lyons argued in an exhaustive essay (1983: 113-44), Playfair was drawing the outline of a very modern debate. And particularly in our times characterized by the expansion of 'knowledge economy' and resultant need for professional/technical education and skilled 'human resources', this debate has acquired added intensity. The idealistic vision of liberal education is in a crisis, and pragmatic interests begin to shape the agenda of higher learning. No wonder, as Clark Kerr (1963) would have argued, the American utilitarian idea of a 'multiversity' as a service-based enterprise specializing in training, research and advice for all major sectors of society is becoming popular throughout the world. The dominant argument is that there should be a closer connection between universities and emerging markets for educated labour.

Yes, these arguments, a pragmatist might argue, have their relevance. Because knowledge cannot be separated from practical interests, and it is also important to train a skilled generation capable of managing the ever-changing techno-economic enterprises. Moreover, one might also smell some sort of intellectual elitism in the classical tradition of liberal education. Yet, I would insist, an educationist like Newman was making a relevant point we should not lose sight of because of our recent enthusiasm for market-friendly education. A university, Newman believed, should cultivate our quest for truth, and a 'cultivated intellect', he was hopeful, would not only serve its own purpose, it would also fulfil a social function. After all, better men, as Newman hoped, make a better world! In other words, a university, no matter how utilitarian it becomes, ceases to be a university if it loses its idealism: its quest for fundamental truth, for beauty, and for the cultivation of human mind. Not the negation of the practical, but the task of elevating it to a higher level of refinement is what should distinguish a university, and separate it from a mere polytechnic or a business school. I would, therefore, celebrate the idea of a university in which 'useful' branches of knowledge like biotechnology, computer science and financial economics are by no means allowed to devalue the significance of, say, a professor contemplating on Tibetan Buddhism, or a scholar offering a course in Sanskrit literature! Let this confluence enrich our understanding, and make us realize that there is also a world beyond immediate practical needs. Otherwise, we are likely to find ourselves in a situation in which, as Ronald Barnett wrote with great concern, 'skills develop; policies are shaped; techniques are refined; but wisdom as a form of deep reflection, collective exchange, and a recognition and even a critique of inner values is put in jeopardy (Barnett 1994: 153).

In India too we find a similar debate, a similar concern. If we look at the social context in which modern universities emerged in colonial India, it is not difficult to understand that a basic purpose behind the establishment of these centres for higher learning, as the Wood's Despatch declared in no uncertain terms, was 'the diffusion of European knowledge'. But a nation that got independence after a prolonged struggle for decolonization was bound to rethink the purpose of higher learning. It was not so much a question of critiquing what the Wood's Despatch celebrated: 'the improved arts, science, philosophy and literature of Europe'. Essentially, it was about an urgent need for consolidating the foundation of a newly independent nation strengthening its techno-industrial infrastructure, and thereby overcoming poverty and inequality. No wonder, the recommendations of the Radhakrishnan Commission (1948–49) reflected rather sharply on the changing conceptions of 'duties and responsibilities of our universities'. Universities, we were told, 'must enable the country to attain, in short a time as possible, freedom from want, disease and ignorance, by the application and development of scientific and technological knowledge' (Quoted in Bhatt and Aggarwal 1969: 98). Yet, these practical needs, as the Commission repeatedly emphasized, would not make much sense without the quest for fundamental values. If in the name of practicality we forget 'higher values of life', the danger is that 'we will have a number of scientists without conscience, technicians without taste who find a void within themselves, a moral vacuum and a desperate need to substitute something, anything, for their lost endeavour and purpose (Ibid: 101). Indeed, it is refreshing to recall that 'we are building a civilization, not a factory or a workshop; and the quality of a civilization depends not on the material equipment or the political machinery but on the character of men' (Ibid: 102-103). See the grandness of the ideal that the Radhakrishnan Commission placed before us:

> We cannot preserve real freedom unless we preserve the value of democracy, justice and liberty, equality and fraternity. It is the ideal towards which we should work though we may be modest in planning our hopes to the result which in the near future are likely to be achieved. 'Utopias are sweet dreams', wrote Kant, but to strive relentlessly towards them is the duty of the citizen and of the statesmen as well. Universities must stand for these ideal causes which can never be lost so long as men seek wisdom and follow righteousness (Ibid: 100-01).

Times are, however, changing fast. And the demand for 'useful' education is becoming more and more intense. As the National Knowledge Commission (2007) states, we need to 'facilitate knowledge applications in sectors like health, agriculture and industry' because 'the ability of a nation to use and create knowledge capital determines its capacity to empower and enable its citizens by increasing human capabilities'. But then, it should never be forgotten that a university, even if it excels in the production of useful knowledges, ceases to be a university if it loses its fundamental queries—its finer ideals of freedom, creativity, and intellectual/moral/spiritual enrichment. How important it is to retain these ideals, particularly at a time when global capitalism seeks to alter the very agenda of education.

II
FRAGMENTS, HIERARCHIES AND BEYOND

The question is: are we actually capable of retaining these ideals? To begin with, let us reflect on the way our orientation to knowledges is undergoing a transformation. It is indeed becoming increasingly difficult to retain a truly holistic or dialogic culture in the university. An important reason is that with modernity, knowledges get increasingly fragmented and specialized. Possibly *reductionism* as an epistemological principle becomes dominant; it is thought that the whole can be reduced into parts, and what is, therefore, important is to study the part, or the fragment with all its details. No wonder, a sense of the whole, or a spirit of connectedness is often sacrificed because of this narrow and over-specialized interest. Modern medicine, to take a specific illustration, reveals rather strikingly the epistemology of reductionism and its implicit over-specialization. A general physician with an understanding of the body as a whole, we all realize, is becoming a rare species; instead, each fragment of the body is now seen as a discrete entity, and subject to the medical gaze of super-specialized doctors. Likewise, in a university we see professors and departments with narrow specialization and rigid disciplinary boundaries. Seldom does one find a situation in which, say, a molecular biologist, a neo-classical economist and a feminist theorist interact, share ideas, and contribute to the understanding of the world in a more holistic and integrated fashion. Indeed, specialization has gone to such an extent that, as a professor of biotechnology once told me, 'even among colleagues in the same department there is hardly any communication'. We all seem to be living in our insulated islands of research. This over-specialization, I guess, has two negative consequences: (a) it leads to some sort of retreat into one's narrow domain of expertise, and this fragmented view of the world further prevents one from developing a broader understanding of the reality; and (b) it promotes and exaggerates the cult of specialized experts, and as a result, the space for public intellectuals and educators tends to get reduced. This is unfortunate. Because, as Henry Giroux (1997) stated with absolute conviction, when we define an academic only through the narrow language of professionalism, we fail to realize that 'teachers as cultural workers should also actively struggle as public intellectuals who can relate to and address wider issues that affect both the immediacy of their location and the wider global context'.

There is yet another important reason for the lack of connectedness or holism in a university. In fact, apart from excessive specialization and its inherent limitations, these multiple disciplines, it seems, are often ranked in a hierarchy. There are two aspects to this hierarchy. First, some branches of knowledge are seen as more 'objective', more 'universal', and hence more 'legitimate' than others. Take, for instance, three main schools in an average university—school of natural sciences, school of social sciences, and school of arts and humanities. It is generally believed that natural sciences have solid foundations; discoveries, laws and theoretical postulates in these sciences are based on hard empirical facts, experimentations and the principle of universal logic that transcend all sorts of socio-cultural barriers and biases, whereas liberal arts and humanities, to take another extreme, are seen as domains of creative imagination, subjectivity and cultural particularism, and hence not 'true' in a way national sciences are. In fact, a distinction is being created between objective science and literary imagination, universalism and particularism, and fact and fiction. Even though contemporary philosophies of science and recent postmodern sensibilities seek to unsettle this distinction,[1] in the actual everyday practice of academic life the rule of the positivist regime and its hierarchies do not wither away easily. Not surprisingly, there is a severe identity confusion or methodological riddle that social sciences experience. Are social sciences, as far as their methodologies are concerned, nearer to natural sciences—their objectivity, universality and value-neutrality? Or, are these sciences more akin to arts and humanities? Yes, those who are still positivists of some sort, and striving for a legitimate scientific status in the domain of knowledge—say, economists or sociologists with a high degree of quantitative techniques—would never feel comfortable with the 'subjectivity' of arts and humanities. With their 'scientificity' they would rather retain a safe distance from literature, metaphysics, philosophy and aesthetics. But then, there are also social scientists who are more hermeneutic and, therefore, more sensitive to the domain of creativity, imagination, reflexivity and understanding. In other words, social sciences are impossible to imagine without this methodological anxiety.

The point that I wish to argue is that these methodological hierarchies prevent the possibility of a respectable and equal relationship among different disciplines. Even if not always articulated explicitly, natural scientists, it may not be entirely wrong to say, see themselves as more legitimate seekers of truth doing something objective and universal. They see themselves as more intelligent, rigorous, specialized, and separated from the vagueness of ethno-knowledge. With this epistemological arrogance, it is not surprising if they look at humanities and social sciences with a sense of ridicule and scepticism. They may allege that people in humanities are making simple things complex; they are essentially esoteric, and not really relevant as far as the practical needs of the world are concerned. Furthermore, their ideas are heavily opinionated without objective foundations! Likewise, scholars of humanities and social sciences become offensive, and accuse natural scientists of their isolation, their ignorance of finer things of life, their conservatism, and above all their apolitical attitude.

> Right from school education one internalizes the hierarchy of knowledges; science, it is thought, is for bright people, whereas humanities are for the rest. A university is not an island. It reproduces the same hierarchy.[2]
>
> I know of a professor of physics who refuses to see any relevance in what I do in the university: teaching Portuguese language and literature. It is sad. I feel that it is important to break the isolation of science. Scientists must know how to communicate with lay persons, and how to understand others.[3]

> Unfortunately, for a scientist, interest in larger issues is seen as a negative quality. It indicates that one is not sufficiently focused, and thereby becoming unnecessarily philistine.[4]

These apprehensions indicate, if I use C.P. Snow's much-talked-about idiom, 'two cultures' (Snow 1964) which continue to prevail in our universities, and cause mutual suspicion, hostility and rigid stereotypes.

The second component of this hierarchy is related to differential prospects and privileges attached to these branches of knowledge. Natural sciences (possibly not 'pure' sciences, but applied, policy-oriented, techno-economic sciences), it would not be wrong to say, have more money, more projects, more opportunities, and hence students in these disciplines are likely to be better placed, whereas social sciences and humanities have perpetual financial insecurity, and students live with terrible anxiety relating to their career prospects. Imagine, for instance, the contrasting self-identity of a student of computer science and, say, a student of Urdu literature. Anyone who has lived in an Indian university knows that these two students, even though belonging to the same institute, live in two different worlds. A budding computer scientist knows that a lucrative career is awaiting him, whereas a student of Urdu literature, even though bright, knows that the future is terribly uncertain, and difficulties are enormous. Look at the gravity of the crisis. A newspaper reports:

> Running a dhaba, a photostat shop or a general store for a living is not what one would have in mind after spending 12 years in academics to get a Ph.D. But that is what a few of the Ph.D. holders from JNU, in Persian and Urdu, have been doing for a living....[5]

Even if these are extreme cases, the fact is that these contrasting worlds with asymmetrical opportunities and resources within the same university cause widespread anguish, and demoralization amongst students and teachers. 'I experience a sense of void', a research student of mine once told me. As he added, 'Many of my friends from economics and other lucrative disciplines are talking about their fat salaries, their new jobs in corporate sectors. But I do not know what would happen after my research, whether I would be fortunate enough to get a job in a college or in a university'. Yes, my student's lonely battle reveals the crisis: how the growing marketization of education does injustice to those who are equally good, bright and sincere, but pursuing a project that, instead of being instrumental, is more philosophical and fundamental. Not solely that. This hierarchy leads the more 'successful' sciences (sciences which are economically beneficial) to retreat into their own privileged world, and as a result, the cohesiveness of the university as an integrated whole gets further eroded. 'Most scientists in these fields', argued Edward Shils, 'have tended not to interest themselves in the university as a whole. For them, the university has become an administrative convenience, a faculty club which is a place for departmental lunches. The central administration is a burden, a token of excessive overhead charges on grants which the individual scientist has acquired through his own exertions outside the university' (Shils 1992: 262). Can we overcome this duality?

Apart from resisting the marketization of education, we also need a more inclusive culture conducive to a meaningful and sustained cross-disciplinary dialogue and conversation in order to retain the grand ideal of higher learning. However, disciplinary boundaries which are retained through specialized journals, professional associations and peer pressure are not always easy to transcend. We all realize how our respective disciplines give us distinctive identities as knowledge seekers (I am a historian, I visit the archives; and you are an anthropologist, you visit the field, and write ethnography; or I am a sociologist, and Durkheim and Weber are my icons; and you are a philosopher, you speak more of Kant and Hegel), and, therefore, an attempt to enter someone else's territory is not easily appreciated. One begins to fear that it would cause identity confusion. Yet, as I wish to argue, it is not altogether impossible to overcome these difficulties. After all, disciplinary boundaries—if we think with an open mind—cannot be said to be very rigid; disciplines often merge and overlap in terms of shared concerns. For instance, I have often wondered whether it would be really feasible for any single discipline to monopolize a thinker like Karl Marx. In Marx's writings and concerns, any careful reader would admit, we see sociology, politics, history, economics and philosophy merging. Or, for that matter, should Sigmund Freud be taught only in the department of psychology? The fact is that Freud's penetrating writings on civilization and moral questions (ranging from *Totem and Taboo* to *Civilization and its Discontents*) have immense relevance to the students of anthropology, sociology and literature. The point I am trying to plead for is that disciplinary boundaries are not made of iron walls; they can be transcended. See the way a professor of economics of education has once narrated the story of this quest:

> It is absolutely important to have a cross-disciplinary dialogue. As an economist, I realize how important it is for economics to interact with sociology, psychology and history to understand people's choices. I know that in my own university there are at least fifteen professors across disciplines who are working on education. But seldom do they interact, and share their ideas. This must stop, and we should strive for a more cross-disciplinary interaction.[6]

Or, think of a professor of literature having a similar quest:

> I work on Latin American Literature I wonder why no communication with scholars of international politics is taking place. After all, Latin American literature reveals the dynamics of polity, economy and culture which should be of interest to them.[7]

This quest, I believe, should be celebrated for both epistemological as well as ethical reasons. The more we learn from one another the more we enlarge our horizon, and overcome our insulation. This dialogic process breaks stereotypes about others; it also generates a sense of humility, and makes one realize that there is a bigger world beyond one's narrow specialization. That is why, natural sciences, social sciences and humanities need to interact more frequently. Take a concrete example. In India we all have witnessed the debate on development which in recent times has gained new momentum because of diverse socio-political and environmental movements, like the *Narmada Bachao Andolan.* I have often felt that a university would be an ideal place for a truly meaningful cross-disciplinary dialogue on development—a dialogue in which, for example, cultural anthropologists working on adivasis and their mode of engagement with nature; environmental scientists studying the ecological implications of developmental projects; economists engaged with cost-benefit analysis; and sociologists reflecting on the social consequences of displacement and homelessness can sit together, share their perspectives, listen to one another, and enrich our understanding. The fact is that development has multiple layers and complex meanings, and a mature cross-disciplinary dialogue enables us to go deeper. It can also make each discipline rethink the kind of questions it raises, and the paradigm it takes for granted.

In this context I wish to make yet another important point. Humanities and social sciences should have the capacity to unite the university as a whole, and give a distinctive character to it. After all, humanities and social sciences are concerned with our collective destiny, and because of their very nature, are capable of arousing the interests of diverse sections of society. Music or poetry; film or aesthetics; religion or politics—if addressed and communicated in an imaginative way—can attract almost everybody in the university. Edward Shils, it seems, captured this spirit when he reflected on 'social science as public opinion' (1977: 273–285). Even quite technical social science, argued Shils, finds its way into broader pools of public opinion. No wonder, even those who study subjects other than social science cannot escape its influence. It is, therefore, necessary and desirable on the part of these departments—social sciences and humanities—to offer carefully designed courses for students of natural sciences, and to organize public lectures and workshops. Let these departments humanize the university, and contribute to the growth of its moral conscience. Ironically, however, this does not happen easily. There are two constraints. First, these departments too fall into the same trap of excessive specialization, and the practitioners of these disciplines begin to fear that a wider dialogue with lay persons would somehow dilute their epistemological foundations, and trivialize their professional identities. Not surprisingly, the humanness of these disciplines gets lost. Because of a strange academic logic of production, dissemination and specialization of knowledge even a literary figure like Premchand, to take an example, gets confined to the ritualism of academics, and becomes merely a Ph.D. topic for students of Hindi literature. Or, for that matter, women's oppression becomes yet another exclusivist theme reserved for an over-specialized gender studies group! The diffusion of ideas, and their liberating potential get blocked as departments lose the thread of connectedness with people's aspirations, and become utterly monopolistic. I am not pleading for populism. Instead, I am arguing that great ideas need not necessarily lose their depth if we start communicating with the larger audience. And it is this art of communication that distinguishes a public intellectual from a mere specialist. Public intellectuals are great educators. Isn't it so revealing that Noam Chomsky is being read by all sorts of people—natural scientists, political activists and university professors; or a political theorist like Rajni Kothari does not remain limited to select departments? A university would lose its beauty if its departments of humanities and social sciences fail to produce public intellectuals.

Second, because of the hierarchy of knowledges I have already referred to, the practitioners of liberal arts and social sciences tend to develop acute anxiety regarding their own location, status and social functions. Possibly this epistemological insecurity further discourages them to live with zeal and enthusiasm. How is it then possible for them to emerge as charismatic leaders and conscience-makers in the university?

As a matter of fact, even in our own university, which has a distinctively rich tradition in social sciences and humanities, there are students and researchers with a wounded consciousness. They experience a crisis of meaning in what they do; and this purposelessness causes helplessness and anguish. However, if we think deeply, we realize that there are deeper purposes that social sciences and humanities can fulfil. Take, for instance, a discipline like sociology which, as some technical experts of 'useful' sciences might allege, is too diffused, too vague and too generalized. But sociology, it has to be realized, has two important functions to fulfil. First, what comes to my mind immediately is something called *secular theology*: an urge to create a better world, and provide new moral foundations of a modern society. In fact, when I look at the intellectual trajectory of some of the finest sociologists of the modern era, I find this common thread in their mission. Auguste Comte—the celebrated sociologist who gave immense momentum to the discipline in the first half of the nineteenth century—was witnessing the new French society caused by the great revolution. It was indeed a world in transition: the old medieval/theological order collapsing, and the new secular/industrial order emerging. And Comte's sociology, we all know, sought to create a 'positive religion of humankind'—a religion uniting science and ethics, and modernity and community—to reconstruct the new society. In a way, Emile Durkheim—yet another French sociologist—inherited the same tradition. He was secular, modern and scientific, yet deeply eager to restore collective order in an industrial society characterized by heightened differentiation, specialization and division of labour. It was like reaffirming the transcendent power of the sacred in an otherwise secular world. And for that matter, even Karl Marx, despite his close affinity with the scientificity of historical materialism, was not merely a dispassionate/detached observer. He too was immensely romantic and spiritual, and guided by the intense passion to create a communist society free from exploitation, fragmentation and alienation. To put it otherwise, the inspiration that we derive from these classical thinkers makes us realize that it is this role of a *visionary* that gives a refreshingly new meaning to the vocation of sociology, or for that matter, to liberal arts and humanities. It is like finding a higher objective in what one does. It is like relating the quest for knowledge to a supreme goal, and living with self-dignity and higher purpose. Second, there is yet another important role—the role of a *critic*—that can be assigned to the practitioners of these disciplines. A critic does not get carried away by the dominant/official ideology; instead, it is the willingness to see alternative ways of looking at the world, and appreciate differences and voices of dissent that distinguishes her. But then, this criticality does not mean that one has to be cynical, and 'deconstruct' everything. A critic, it should not be forgotten, is also striving for something positive and humane. In fact, this role of a critic can be seen in the intellectual mission of some of our creative social scientists who are interrogating the status quo—say, a mode of ruthless techno-industrial development, or a consumptionist/patriarchical structure with gender stereotypes and inequalities, and at the same time, striving for an egalitarian, inclusive and ecologically sensitive society.

In other words, humanities and social sciences can take us beyond 'instrumental' interests, and make us realize the significance of what Habermas would have regarded as 'hermeneutic' and 'emancipatory' interests in the quest for knowledge (Habermas 2004). That is why, as I am arguing, these branches of knowledge ought to play a leading role in restoring the holistic/humanistic ideal of the university, and generating a higher purpose to bring sanity in an otherwise over-specialized academic arena with rigid boundaries, divisions and hierarchies.

III
TEACHING AND RESEARCH: TOWARDS A SYMMETRY

What about a symmetrical relationship between teaching and research—yet another important ideal that a university ought to uphold? Teaching is essentially about the transmission of knowledges and ideas; it is an act of communion with a new generation of learners. And research is about one's perpetual alertness: one's eagerness to explore the ever-expanding frontiers of knowledge. In fact, the ideal of a university is that one is continually exploring new ideas through research, and also sharing and communicating these discoveries and innovations with young minds. A university faculty ought to be a thinker as well as a communicator, a researcher as well as a teacher. As a teacher, I myself realize this truth every day. For example, I teach a course on *Modern Indian Social Thought*, and when I deliver a series of lectures on Gandhi, I realize how difficult the task is. I just can't come to the class, and repeat the age-old stereotypes about Gandhi. I am required to go deeper; it is necessary on my part to see how social philosophers and activists of diverse ideological traditions—Ambedkarites, subalternists, eco-feminists and postcolonial theorists—have engaged with Gandhi. In other words, delivering a lecture on Gandhi is like doing a research on a series of complex texts: from B.R.Ambedkar's *What Congress and Gandhi have done to the Untouchables* to Ashis Nandy's *The Intimate Enemy*. Teaching and research are indeed difficult to separate.

> Research itself is the methodical acquisition of knowledge, hitherto unknown. Knowledge languishes and fades if it is not cultivated research. Teaching too languishes if it is not sustained by research. Even though a particular teacher himself does relatively little research, he has to be informed about the research which is being done on his subject. Knowledge is not self-sustaining; it does not grow of itself. It has to be actively sought and brought into teaching to remain alive. These are among the first responsibilities of the academic (Shils 1982: 113).

Yes, it is indeed a great ideal. One is striving for new ideas, and one is also creating a new generation of learners. What else can be more demanding? Yet, as I wish to argue, it is not always easy to retain this symmetry. A major reason, I believe, lies in a new hierarchy which, even though not always stated openly, implies that teaching is somehow less prestigious than research—at least, for the academic profile of a university faculty. Why is it so? Research, we all realize, has a distinctively higher ideal: raising new questions and striving for appropriate answers, and moreover, retaining a high degree of intellectual zeal, perseverance, and absolute dedication to the domain of knowledge. It is in this sense that research—or the quest for new knowledge—leads one to go beyond oneself, and pursue an ideal that transcends what can be regarded as immediate/utilitarian aspects of university life: coming to the department, doing the routine work, retaining the job, and earning the salary! Great researchers with their dedication and path-breaking publications arouse immense dynamism, inspire students, and take the university to a higher level of excellence. In comparison to this noble ideal of research, teaching may be perceived—particularly, by those who see it from outside—as relatively less stimulating and demanding. They may see it as just another everyday engagement—coming to the class, delivering the lecture, relying on already prescribed select texts, completing the syllabus, conducting the examination, and grading the students. It does not require extraordinary scholarship; it requires just moderate intelligence and some sort of communicative skill. Teachers, unlike researchers, do not generate new ideas!

I, however, wish to interrogate this perception. First, I would examine the negative consequences of this hierarchy—the way the special emphasis which is put on research publications (publish or perish) has led to the negation of the grand ideal of research, and also caused its trivialization. Second, I would argue that meaningful teaching, unlike what outsiders think of it, is an immensely creative act which is also a kind of research in its own distinctive way, and without which a university becomes utterly dull and colourless—devoid of a stimulating exchange of ideas.

It is indeed important to examine the way research itself is losing its purity, and is being projected as a kind of attractive package that sells in these pragmatic times. What becomes important is not necessarily the authenticity of one's fundamental quest, but how one's research gets instant visibility, how it brings money, consultancy and projects, and how it is concretized through widespread social networking. In a country like ours this problem has acquired yet another dimension. To put it without much pretence, it is almost an obsessive preoccupation with foreign connections and foreign publications. If you are 'somebody', you must visit abroad (I mean Euro-American universities) frequently; you must have somebody out there whom you can occasionally invite to your own department. And you must develop a particular idiom—your 'subalternity' must be sold in American universities; your 'cultural studies' must be 'Sanskritized' through select quotes from Walter Benjamin and Michel Foucault; and amongst your

Indian colleagues you must away remember with great nostalgia: 'When I was at Oxford....' This mindset has entered so deep into our consciousness that the other day a student of mine asked me without the slightest hesitation: 'Sir, what are you doing here in this terrible summer when many of your colleagues are visiting Europe and delivering lectures?' I do not blame my student. He is only revealing the trend. He knows that research must sell, and glamorize itself.

And the irony is that this sort of research is often being privileged and awarded. A striking illustration of this unethical practice is the way some of the leading universities in India are appointing professors. Insiders know how, at times, one gets direct professorship simply because one has visibility in terms of research with appropriate social/cultural capital, and 'right' publications in 'right' places. Even if one does not have adequate teaching experience it does not matter. In fact, a hierarchy has already been established in our leading universities: there are some who are supposedly great researchers, who are tremendously mobile, visit abroad frequently, write papers in international journals, bring projects, and place their research students in appropriate places; and there are others who are simply invisible, who just teach in silence and wait endlessly for their promotions. This hierarchical practice has not done good to the culture of the university. It is not difficult to come across college/university teachers expressing their utter anguish and discontent:

> Imagine my case. I have to teach fourteen hours a week. I have to supervise M.Phil/Ph.D. students. See the amount of work I do. It is, however, sad that for the selection committee, teaching has no worth, no significance.[8]
>
> Essentially, it is a matter of one's value and choice: whether one likes classroom interaction, feedback from students, and satisfaction in teaching; or whether one wants to become 'big' instantly by publishing as much as one can. But we all know that at the end of the day one's 'worth' would be measured solely in terms of one's publications.[9]

In this context it is also important to realize that the very logic of quantification (number of books, papers and conferences) is doing severe damage to the dignity of research and quality of publications. Apart from the terrible psychic stress one undergoes, it leads to the trivialization of publications. In natural sciences it is more like what Thomas Kuhn would have regarded as 'puzzle solving' exercises based on the dominant paradigm of one's chosen discipline. These publications need not necessarily demonstrate one's creativity. Publications, as a professor of biotechnology once shared with me, are often routinized. 'The more you publish the more projects you get. The more projects you get the more you publish'. Likewise, in social sciences, a careful look at the accelerated growth of the industry of edited volumes (and even some of the prestigious publication houses are engaged in this business), and journals (even the so-called 'refereed' journals) does indicate that, barring exceptions, most of these publications are not really contributing to the domain of knowledge in any significant way. In fact, if one dares to see beyond the trap of words (often borrowed from the likes of Bourdieu and Focault) with ornamental footnotes and references, or statistical details (further mystified through sophisticated quantitative techniques), one realizes how one publication leads to another, and at the end of the day we all are caught into this fetish: the mindless game of ceaselessly demonstrating our 'academic productivity'. To quote a leading Indian academic:

> Creativity can be destroyed by boxing it into rigid compartments or by creating hierarchies or by pronouncing judgements prematurely or by imposing quantitative criteria. For instance, in the chase to publish (or perish), often a researcher has little time to work through his ideas completely. A system which imposes quantitative criterion of publications for evaluation dooms itself to mediocrity, to narrowness of linear ideas...So often in physics or economics, a publication is not even a new idea but merely a change in some parameter or another way of generating a stable state etc...In economics very often papers are also divorced from any reality. Often enough it almost appears that a second rate mathematician or a physicist would have done a better job of building such an economic model, and yet such an economist would do

exceedingly well as an economist in today's environment (Kumar 1989: 135–36).

This is not to suggest that everybody has become a smart player of this game, and every piece of research is necessarily shallow or ornamental. There are scholars amongst us who do meaningful research, and generate new ideas. Their publications, far from being routinized, open up the window, and expand our horizon. For example, if we take the domain of social science research, Indian universities have indeed been enriched by historians like Bipan Chandra and Irfan Habib, or sociologists like M.N. Srinivas and A.R. Desai. In fact, similar illuminating stories, I am sure, would emerge from every discipline. This ideal of creative research has to be perpetually asserted. Not simply because there are inauthentic researchers amongst us, but also because an average Indian university is otherwise full of teachers who seldom publish research papers. We need an environment that encourages research.

In this context I wish to make another important point. Teaching itself loses its creativity if it is not in constant touch with research. Well, it is always possible to find teachers who do not take their jobs seriously. It is true that they do not inspire, do not generate new ideas, and just dictate notes, and somehow complete the syllabus. And it is also possible that students are not interested in rigorous learning, and they expect nothing beyond what exams—yes, a faulty pattern of exams—demand from them. This vicious circle seems to have reduced the act of teaching into a dull/monotonous affair. No wonder, one often feels tempted to conclude that a researcher is inherently superior to a teacher. However, anyone who has taught—and taught with a lot of rigour, enthusiasm and intensity—in a college/university knows fairly well that teaching, contrary to the prevalent stereotype, requires tremendous mental energy: working with students, arousing their curiosity, and inviting them to new ideas and challenges emerging in the discipline. It is in this sense that a good teacher is also a good researcher. Even if she is not a researcher in terms of visibility, she is perpetually exploring ideas, reading new books, and expanding her horizon. Even today, despite multiple constraints, there are many bright teachers working in silence. And I have always felt that it is because of their dedication—the way they teach and disseminate new ideas—all celebrity researchers have acquired their legitimacy. Foucault is Foucault, or, for that matter, Andre Beteille is Andre Beteille precisely because their ideas are being taught, discussed and disseminated in the classroom. Indeed, the silent work of great teachers and the fame of creative researchers are inseparable. Moreover, one who loves teaching often realizes that some of the finest moments of creativity and intellectual stimulation emerge in the classroom itself: when students make observations and raise penetrating questions. It is this classroom dialogue that often gives one an idea to explore further, to write a paper or a book. Teaching, in other words, encourages research, and research makes teaching complete. 'For every lecture I deliver', a bright young professor of literature once told me, 'there is a great deal of research; I have to read new books, acquaint myself with new ideas'. There is no exaggeration in this argument. Listening to an illuminating and inspiring lecture delivered by a professor, every good student would agree, is like reading a good book, and celebrating every part of it with great joy and enthusiasm. Not solely that. Good teaching is endowed with immense moral potential. After all, it is democratic and communicative. It begins with an urge to share, and interact with young minds. As a process, it is perpetually refreshing; it blooms every day. What else is a university without a vibrant community of teachers and students evolving an intimate bond?

IV
PRAXIS OF LEARNING

A university is also a place that ought to emerge as a model: a model inspiring an alternative culture, a new possibility. True, a university is not an island; students and teachers bring with them their cultural beliefs, practices and prejudices. Yet, it is legitimate to expect that a university, precisely because it is a reflexive community of thinkers and researchers engaged with ideas, should interrogate many ugly and oppressive beliefs and practices which are otherwise prevalent in the larger society, and generate alternative possibilities. It is in this context that the relationship between theory and practice needs to be reflected on.

A university may be known for its theoretical richness—say, the ideas it generates on class struggle, subaltern voices, women's movements, and environmental consequences of massive developmental projects. However, the moot question is: does the knowledge one acquires in a university actually alter one's mode of living? Or, is it merely an intellectual exercise? I would rather argue that a university can exist as a model for the rest of society only when it seeks to evolve a symmetry between theory and practice, knowing and doing, and intellect and wisdom. Certainly, it is a difficult ideal. For example, it may not be particularly easy for a bright professor of politics to declass himself, and give up his bourgeois habits, even if he is inclined to Marxism. Or, for that matter, a professor of environmental sciences may not be willing to minimize the use of AC cars. Nor is it convenient for a feminist theoretician to give freedom to a modern *dasi*: a female domestic help who keeps 'cooking, sweeping, cleaning'—an activity that the agenda of women's liberation would hardly approve of. Likewise, a typical university seminar on Gandhi might not hesitate to spend a huge amount of money on butter chicken and whisky. This gap should by no means negate the contributions that these scholars otherwise make to the understanding of politics, gender, environment and even Gandhi's truth. After all, a university should also be known for its relatively autonomous theoretico-philosophical quest. Nevertheless, it is always desirable to try, to evolve a sensitivity: a willingness to bring one's life relatively closer to what one learns or teaches. Otherwise, the gap between theory and practice, I fear, would dishonour theory itself. Imagine a university in which professors choose to avoid cars, and instead, use bicycles or simply walk while moving around the campus; students refuse to engage in matrimonial alliances involving dowry, and the entire community pledges to free the campus from polythene and plastic. Possibly such a dream university would give birth to an altogether different notion of excellence: not just in terms of publications, academic honours and international ranking, but essentially in terms of the quality of life a university nurtures, or its ability to make a significant difference in people's life-practices. Only then would theoretical discourses on global warming, environmental crisis and patriarchal violence acquire their legitimacy.

There is yet another dimension to our quest for an alternative culture. Can universities decolonize our consciousness? The transaction of ideas and knowledges is not always symmetrical. It would not be wrong to say that Euro-American universities continue to exist as our reference points. The books we read, the journals we prefer, the theories we adhere to, the icons we worship—the West seems to be everywhere. It becomes exceedingly difficult to decolonize our consciousness, to have faith in ourselves, and to acquire the courage to find alternative sources of knowledge. How often we have seen our students reading everything about Habermas and his understanding of modernity, but remaining altogether ignorant of Sri Aurobindo's *The Human Cycle:* the text that too reflects on modernity or the 'age of reason' and its discontents. Likewise, we find students working on the specificity of Indian history/social reality, yet desperate to join any Euro-American university to complete their doctoral works. Decolonization of consciousness, let me assert once again, does not mean boycotting the West or its academic discourses. Its only meaning is openness: a creative/reflexive attitude that gives us the strength—epistemological and cultural—to negotiate with the West as an equal partner. This means cultivating our own resources—our own centres, our own journals, our own traditions of enquiry, and our own vocabulary. We, however, fail because we are not making any sustained effort to alter the prevalent asymmetry. And, instead, we are planning to invite foreign universities.

Even though we live in terribly hard/pragmatic times, and Utopias disappear fast, there are flashes of truth that keep the search for a new culture alive. The other day while I was entering the university to take my class, I happened to meet a student of mine who had sat with Medha Patkar on a hunger strike to express his solidarity with the *Narmada Bachao Andolan*. I saw light in his face, and I immediately realized that this time when I would deliver a lecture on Antonio Gramsci (an 'organic intellectual', said Gramsci, is not just a man of letters, but essentially an active participant in practical life as a constructor, organizer and permanent persuader), I would feel more confident because I could convince my students of the real presence of organic intellectuals amongst us. Or, for that matter, when George W. Bush was visiting India, I saw a carnival of protest in our university which, in fact, inspired the anti-imperialism campaign in the capital. These were indeed great moments of hope.

How nice it is to recall that it is in the university that I have seen a living protest against patriarchy. I have seen a more healthy and egalitarian relationship between men and women; I have felt the fresh air of freedom: women moving around freely, articulating their worldviews, taking major decisions, and choosing their life-projects. It is in the university that I have seen cross-cultural marriages, sensitivity to animal rights, and growing environmental consciousness. I have also witnessed a history of resistance—students and teachers struggling, suffering and articulating their voices of dissent against the terror of Emergency Mrs. Indira Gandhi imposed in 1975; their active participation in the relief work after the Bhopal gas tragedy; and their remarkable role in restoring communal harmony in the capital after the riots in 1984. It is only in such a university that one day I could come to the class, and instead of delivering a formal lecture on the prescribed syllabus, ask a student to read a passage from Dostoyevsky's *The Dream of a Ridiculous Man*: a man who in his fantasy entered a new world, and described its people in such a vivid manner:

> They desired nothing and were content, they did not strive to know life the way we strive to probe its depth, because their life was consummate. Their knowledge was finer and more profound than our science, for our sincere attempts to explain the meaning of life. Science itself strives to fathom it in order to teach others how to live; while they know how to live without the help of science. I saw it but I could not understand

> this knowledge of theirs. They showed their trees to me, and I failed to appreciate the depth of the love with which they gazed at them; it was as if they were speaking to beings like themselves. And do you know, I may not be wrong if I tell you that they did speak to them. Yes, they had found a common tongue and I am convinced the trees understood them. This was the way they treated all Nature—the beasts who lived in peace with them, never attacking them, and loving them, captivated by the people's love for them. They pointed out the stars to me and spoke to me about them, saying things I could not understand, but I am positive they had some tie with those heavenly bodies, a living tie, not spiritual alone (Dostoyevsky 1983: 360-61).

Yes, that day my students forgot formal/academic sociology, and got themselves involved with Dostoyevsky. As I saw their willingness to engage with the 'ridiculous man', I experienced the beauty of the university—its willingness to imagine alternatives, and respect Utopias as future possibilities.

But then, as my more worldly friends would caution me, there are limits to what I can expect from a university. After all, a university is an integral part of this world: a world characterized by the ethos of global capitalism and its market-driven culture. As students and teachers we are not free from our middle class aspirations and anxieties. Is it, therefore, surprising that if, instead of striving for a counter-culture, these days we begin to think more of safe and secure careers, campus recruitment cells, close ties with the corporate world, and marketization of courses? Or, is it surprising that at the end of the day even some of our ultra-leftist students choose to settle down in the United States? Under these circumstances, where is then, as Niblett expressed with great concern, 'a widened and depended awareness, and a sense of direction for human life?' Instead, the emerging trend is bound to alarm us:

> Higher education has in fact tended to become more and more instrumental in character, and even if it includes training in interpersonal skills, more and more subtly so. If its only significant aim is to produce and equip professionals to run with smoothness a managerial, electronic and consumer

> oriented society, what reason is there to think that such a society will take us in the long run where we really want to be?...The more that men or women go on simply using technological devices as ends in themselves or go on being hung up by them, the more the motive for living a life that has scope or depth is weakened. Why should clever animals who can calculate how their appetites can most deliciously be satisfied want to stay human? (Niblett 1994: 115-16)

We should, however, try to resist it. Although philosophers have interpreted the world in many ways, the central task, as Karl Marx reminded us in one of his theses on Feuerbach, is to change it. Even if this Marxian slogan sounds too polemical, these days we have seen a new epistemological sensitivity emerging from the philosophy of science itself. We are told to break the wall that separates the knower from the known, and celebrate the principles of inter-connectedness, holism and compassion. Indeed, the challenge is to keep this quest alive. And herein lies the relevance of the praxis of learning.

V
THE CRISIS AND MYTH OF MARKETIZATION

At this juncture, another important question arises: where do we situate an average Indian university in this entire debate? In almost every domain of social life, India, we know, lives in two different worlds. Even in the field of higher education there is severe inequality. True, we have select universities and institutes gifted with a team of extraordinarily reputed faculty, high quality research, and a vibrant culture of learning. However, here is a country which at the same time has been witnessing a sort of 'diploma disease': proliferation of overcrowded colleges/universities whose only function, it seems, is to conduct examinations throughout the year, distribute degrees/diplomas, and create an illusion of learning. Poor infrastructure, mass copying, irrelevant curriculum, lumpenization, campus violence, and widespread demotivation among students as well as teachers tend to characterize these universities. Neither creative research, nor meaningful teaching: there is absolute trivialization of university degrees. A leading

Indian sociologist could not hide his despair while reflecting on the prevalent chaos:

> Institutions of higher learning today are symbols of indiscipline. Student indiscipline was followed by non-teaching staff indiscipline, and even the teachers have joined forces with these indisciplined sectors. Who should assume the responsibility for setting things right? It sounds harsh but is nonetheless true that a sizeable section of the teaching community does not take its obligation to the students seriously. Teaching is often reduced to an uninspired routine. There is little evidence of renovation of and innovations in instructional methods at a time when first generation learners are entering the portals of higher education in increasing numbers (Dubey1989:171).

How to overcome this depressing scenario? One opinion—and which has gained immense momentum in our times—is that these state-funded universities are fast losing their significance and, therefore, private initiatives need to be encouraged to make higher learning more relevant and meaningful. In the era of economic liberalization, such a viewpoint acquires legitimacy because it is taken for granted that privatization would invariably lead to efficiency; students and teachers would be compelled to become accountable; and courses would, therefore, become truly relevant, and succeed in preparing university graduates for skilled jobs in the expanding market of global capitalism. In fact, what is popularly known as the 'Birla-Ambani Committee Report'[10] states this viewpoint rather sharply. 'A market-oriented competitive environment', we are told, 'is vital for our future'. As we are required to create 'millions of knowledge-based human resources', we need a 'revolution', not reforms. And this revolution, it is stated without any ambiguity, demands 'privatization'. It is, therefore, important to legislate a 'Private University Bill, particularly in the fields of science and technology, management and financial areas'. Not solely that. As the Committee suggests, it is high time we allowed 'foreign direct investment in education'. A perspective of this kind, needless to add, speaks the language of utility, and at a time when Indian universities are in a crisis, it has its appeal, particularly to the aspiring class willing to 'invest for future'. What, however, it fails to take into account is a series of ethical and pedagogical issues relating to the marketization of higher learning. For example, if the state begins to retreat, and allows private enterprises to dictate the agenda of education, it is bound to get further commodified, and become terribly costly. Even if there are provisions for few scholarships, it would invariably favour the privileged sections, and further intensify the already existing inequality in our society. Is there any other possibility left when, to take a revealing example, a leading private university indicates the emerging trend by proudly declaring its course fees: MBBS-Rs. 19,34,500; BDS-Rs. 11,97,500; BE-Rs. 6,03,500; B.Pharm-Rs. 4,83,500; Biotechnology-Rs.3,77,500; Hotel Management-Rs. 6,34,500; B.Sc. Animation-Rs. 6,17,500?[11] Furthermore, as the rationale of the market becomes predominant, it begins to cause severe damage to the quest for fundamental knowledges. Because it would not be an exaggeration to say that private universities and colleges are concentrating primarily on those courses which are saleable, and promise instant job opportunities to their clients. Information technology, biotechnology, tourism, fashion designing, computer science and hotel management—these are courses that occupy the centre-stage, and the other branches of knowledge like theoretical sciences, liberal arts and humanities get more and more marginalized[12]. While this sort of education satisfies the expanding corporate world and aspiring middle class, it devalues the depth of higher learning. I am not suggesting that there is something called 'pure' knowledge which is entirely free from all practical/mundane interests. Every branch of knowledge has practical implications for the concrete/tangible world we live in. Can physics be altogether separated from engineering, history from tourism industry, and sociology from industrial management? Even some academics might feel that this linkage is productive, and, therefore, all over the world there is a pressure from within to marketize education. Derek Bok has rightly captured this mindset:

> Individual faculty members, especially in the best universities, found new ways to supplement their incomes with lucrative activities on the side. As biotechnology boomed, life scientists not only started to seek patents on their discoveries and take attractive consulting assignments; they also began to receive stock from new firms eager for their help and even to found new companies based on their new discoveries. Outside the sciences, business school professors travelled to corporations willing to pay substantial sums for days spent consulting or teaching their executives. Legal scholars began to collect large fees for advising law firms on their corporate clients. Economists, political scientists, psychologists, and many others discovered that their counsel was worth a tidy sum to companies, consulting firms, and other private organizations (Bok 2003:13).

Yet, no matter how tempting this endeavour is, knowledge, it has to be realized, is not just what sells. Physics, history sociology: all these fundamental disciplines have their inherent depth, and if a university loses this sense of depth and beauty in the name of utility, it becomes merely a marketplace which, as Bok cautioned, would eventually damage the academic community. Because it is quite natural that 'professors who work hard at their traditional academic disciplines will resent the extra income earned by colleagues who start a new business or spend a lot of time consulting'; or, for that matter, 'scientists may bridle at the secrecy imposed by a colleague in their department who is funded by a corporation' (Ibid: 113). In other words, the university would begin to decline as a cohesive moral community.

In this context it is also important to rethink the very notion of 'relevance'. What is relevant for the market, let it be realized, need not necessarily be relevant for the larger society. Or, for that matter, what is relevant for people need not be useful for the market. Moreover, what is relevant for the market need not necessarily have the philosophic depth that the university ought to strive for.. Take an example. *Fashion Technology* as a course is indeed relevant for the emerging market, particularly because there is an accelerated growth of consumerism; and the alliance of global capitalism and culture industry, we know, is engaged in manufacturing all sorts of mythical images of fashion and beauty to persuade its target audience. No wonder, *Fashion Technology* as a course has its adherents. It promises job, money and glamour. But then, does a course of this kind truly enhance our sensitivity to art and aesthetics—the way, say, Jamini Roy's paintings or Satyajit Ray's films do? Or, does it generate some kind of liberating consciousness for people to come out of their suffering and servitude? In contrast, think of a rigorous course in *art and aesthetics* which is indeed capable of equipping its learners with appropriate skills as well as critical sensibility: the ability to understand and appreciate how diverse forms of art articulate the changing trajectory of history, and its societal/cultural practices. For example, when a student of mine chooses to write his doctoral thesis on the folklore of Mithila, he conveys a message: even if his thesis does not assure him a job with a fat salary, the university must give him adequate space to go ahead with his project. I have always believed that it is this creative madness that helps the university to retain a safe distance from the market and its aggression. Likewise, there are branches of knowledge—say, *gender studies*—which may not be market-friendly, but may have immense liberating potential. Unlike a course in fashion technology, it may give us penetrating insights into the construction of gender identities, and the power discourse of patriarchy; it can inspire young minds to alter their life-projects, and move towards a just society. A university, I repeat, must celebrate these courses (even if not particularly market-friendly) which have immense philosophic depth and liberating potential. I am not saying that fashion technology or hotel management has to be treated like a pollutant; it has its uses and adherents. But then, if their logic—the logic of immediate utility—colonizes the sphere of learning, there is a danger. Imagine a situation in which our 'bright products' are trained to know only about computer, management and commerce, but not anything significant about physics, literature and social science. It is indeed terrifying, even though they would be earning fat salaries. Social illiteracy amidst technical literacy negates critical and reflexive imagination, and produces a generation which is utterly conformist to the status quo.

Another consequence of commodification is that it is creating a mindset that is affecting the entire ethos of learning. Even state-funded reputed central universities are experiencing this change. For example, in a well-known central university in the capital, one notices how youngsters—particularly after the board examination—get depressed, if they cannot get into commerce or economics! As a matter of fact, a sort of hierarchy of knowledges is deeply internalized, and all that does not sell in the market, be it physics or literature, is seen as 'irrelevant'. Not surprisingly, we are witnessing massive demoralization among students who feel that they are at 'wrong' places and situated in 'wrong' departments. This demotivation, every insider knows, manifests itself in empty classrooms because of poor attendance, in the popularity of 'Champion' guide books,[13] or in the restlessness they show in doing what, they believe, is more important than formal academics: joining a coaching centre for medical/engineering/management entrance test, or for that matter, taking up a job in a call centre!

This has also led to some sort of gendered orientation to knowledges. My own experience suggests that even in a university like ours, liberal arts, humanities, and social sciences are fast becoming predominantly women's subjects. There has been a steady retreat of men from these courses. Is it because in a patriarchal society men feel the extra burden of earning, and thereby 'non-profitable' disciplines fail to attract them? Or, is it because 'hard' techno-economic sciences are seen as more 'rational' and 'masculinist', whereas 'emotive/irrational' women are more akin to 'soft' liberal arts, humanities and cultural studies? Whatever be the reason, the fact is that we are experiencing asymmetry and imbalance in the entire culture of higher learning. It would not be wrong to say that there is immense pressure of marketization and commodification, and the entire curriculum, we are told, must alter its priorities. If we look at the following table, we can understand, as Ronald Barnett has demonstrated with great concern, how the agenda of higher education is getting shifted from the left-hand column to the right-hand column:

knowing-that	knowing-how
internal	external
intellectual	physical
thought	action
problem-making	problem-solving
knowledge as process	knowledge as product
understanding	information
concept-based	task based
pure	applied
disinterested	pragmatic
intrinsic orientation	instrumental orientation
	(Barnett 1994: 48-49)

VI
MODES OF CREATIVE INTERVENTION

The fact is that the market cannot save the domain of higher education. Instead, it further intensifies the crisis. It transforms us into consumers; it seeks to alter the very character of a university—its relatively autonomous domain of free enquiry. This critique does by no means suggest that we should continue to give our consent to the way state-funded average Indian colleges/universities are functioning. As I have already stated, education is in a deep crisis in these centres, and we must intervene. It is in this context that I wish to make three concrete proposals:

Restructuring the curriculum

Academic depth, let it be realized, is by no means the negation of practical knowledge. In fact, what should distinguish it is precisely this confidence: an attempt to overcome all constructed dualities like theory and practice, contemplative knowledge and practical action, and philosophic maturity and vocational skill. It is this integral/holistic orientation which, I believe, should give us the strength to restructure the curriculum, and create a generation of learners for whom academic knowledge, far from remaining merely an ornament, gets concretized in the domain of vocational activities. In order to substantiate my arguments I wish to take three specific cases.

First, look at *sociology*—the discipline I am reasonably familiar with It is not at all uncommon to find undergraduate/postgraduate students of sociology feeling the irrelevance of all that they are doing. It is often said that the existing courses are too theoretical and too bookish to enable them to make sense of the world they live in. See the way a former undergraduate student of sociology from St. Xavier's College, Mumbai, expressed her anguish:

> What remains uncontested is the thorough lack of research and field experience imperative to the learning of social sciences. Not only does the textbook emerge as the fundamental reference point for exam evaluation, it remains the exclusive teaching/learning apparatus to the aid of the educators/students. What is implied is a learnt dependence on the textbook alone with the complete absence of any allied research work on the part of the individual student. Herein lies the fundamental drawback of undergraduate teaching—the teaching of a science devoid of imagination, an exercise in text memorization.[14]

Nor do these courses, as the argument goes, give them the practical skills which are useful for finding appropriate careers and vocations. That is why, the question arises: is it possible to make a course in sociology which is relevant in the sense that while retaining its philosophic/academic depth, it also equips them with meaningful skills and capabilities? This, I believe, is possible provided we are determined to innovate. Think of an undergraduate course in sociology. Yes, it is absolutely important for the students to become familiar with the discipline itself, its origin and evolution, and its diverse methodologies and theoretical perspectives. With this sound sociological imagination, let them enter the domain of Indian sociology: its engagement with caste, community and religion; modernization and development; social movements and social transformation. This theoretical/substantial literature—ranging from the classics written by Durkheim/Weber/Marx to the sociologies of Ghurye, Srinivas and A.R. Desai—ought to be seen as a critical minimum (or core material) that every student must be familiar with. Once this background is developed, it becomes absolutely important to make them learn how this sociological sensibility can be operationalized in practical domains of work—say, how to make a documentary film on female infanticide, or how to write an extensive report on development and displacement; or how to engage in a communicative interaction with slum dwellers, and initiate an awareness programme on the abuses of alcoholism. This is possible if a significant component of college life (say, at least one year) is devoted to truly substantial field training: working with a media house, or the ministry of rural development, or even a school. I would argue that such a pedagogy of *learning through doing* would give a refreshingly new meaning to academic knowledge. Foucault or Habermas would then no longer appear as distant/esoteric names for enhancing one's cultural capital; students would, in fact, begin to learn how to use their critical and creative insights in practical domains of work. Furthermore, with such a renovated course structure and pedagogy, they would also find a meaning and relevance in their studies, and above all, gain the much needed self-confidence: the ability to relate education to the sphere of work. How wonderful it would be to find fresh sociology graduates working as media professionals, or research workers in the planning commission, or even documentary film makers. Not solely that. It would also give them the necessary wisdom—how to contextualize the acquired skill, and use it creatively and productively for the benefit of the larger society. Sociology as a discipline would overcome its stigmatized identity (how often it is being perceived as a 'soft' option—a mix of common sense and newspaper editorials—that can fetch one a degree without much hard work), and appeal to young learners.

Second, take *Hindi literature*—yet another course which, any college student would tell us, is often degraded, condemned and stigmatized. And even those who are opting for this course are almost compelled to feel that what they are doing has no relevance, no prospect. It is really sad. Even though *English literature* has its glamour, Hindi is not regarded as prestigious. Possibly even in a postcolonial society like ours English continues to retain its aura; or possibly as the market expands, English is being seen as some sort of 'cultural capital' for entering the world of trade, commerce and professions. But then, Hindi is our language; it has its distinctive tradition; and no society can excel if it devalues its language and literature. Hindi literature ought to be seen as an important component of the body of knowledge that the university should uphold. It is, however, possible to redesign the entire curriculum. Well, I would argue—and argue strongly—that literature with its great poetry, short stories, novels and dramas is worth studying in its own right. How can we elevate our consciousness and humanize our civilization without literature? Nirala's poetry, Premchand's novels and Hazari Prasad Diwedi's essays require no utility certificate. But then, while enriching this literary sensibility, it is also possible for a course of this kind to make students familiar with contemporary concerns in which language/communicative skills are in great demand. While making such an effort, I am aware, a delicate balance has to be maintained. It is certainly not the task of a course in literature to make students learn, say, how to communicate as a radio jockey on FM channel, or how to impress the audience as a television anchor, or how to write a script for a formula Bollywood film. Yet, at the same time it is not impossible for a student with great literary sensibility to make a difference in journalism, or to write a meaningful script for a film that has also immense mass appeal. It is, therefore, important that together with theories of literary criticism, grammar, linguistics and literary creations, students are also asked to study—and with equal seriousness—carefully designed papers on journalism, script writing, translation, editing and publishing. If they become editors/publishers, script writers, media persons, translators and interpreters, these professions, I must add, would acquire a new meaning and depth. Let Hindi literature as a discipline revitalize itself, and contribute meaningfully to the functioning of diverse vocations many of our students strive for.

And finally, I wish to refer to a positive experimentation that the University of Delhi has made in recent times while introducing an undergraduate course in education. Yes, the *Bachelor of Elementary Education (B.El. Ed)* Programme is a move towards the creation of a cadre of Elementary Education Professionals. In a way it promises the kind of integral holism I am talking about. It is a course that seeks to reconcile fairly developed theories of education and pedagogy with vocational skills that a schoolteacher is required to evolve and sharpen. A rigorous course of this kind that gives great importance to real experiences with the lived reality of school children, school texts and classroom transactions does indeed succeed in giving a sense of purpose to its students. Moreover, teaching as a vocation also acquires a new meaning, and students begin to realize that it is my no means a 'soft' option; instead, like medicine and engineering, it too requires sustained effort, philosophic maturity, exposure to child psychology, sociology of education and politics of curriculum, and above all, everyday engagement with school children. The course is indeed a mature effort to unite critical sensibility with vocationalism.

All these three examples are related to humanities and social sciences. There is a conscious motive behind this choice. Pragmatists and utilitarians, we know, often allege that these disciplines are losing their relevance. I am, however, refuting their arguments, and instead, pleading for the art of new possibilities. These courses with a restructured curriculum and creative pedagogy can make a difference, generate a sense of purpose among students, and relate knowledges to professional experiences. It is obvious that similar experimentations can be done in the other disciplines too, be it physics or mathematics, geography or history.

Today all over the world, because of the growing needs of the corporate economy, its service sector and its expanding market, colleges/universities are experiencing severe pressure. Evolve a relationship with the market, get sponsors, manage your own resources, introduce self-financing courses, and lure students by promising them immediate placement and fat salary—no college/university in the world can escape the pressure of this dictum. How do we cope with it? One way is to accept our defeat easily, surrender the very ideals of higher learning, and go in for complete commodification of education. Another way is to pretend that our colleges/universities can remain as they are: with the same old curriculum and the same mode of teaching. But it would invite only stagnation, and, therefore, further promote the cult of marketization as a remedy to all evils. Beyond these two options, as I am arguing, lies yet another possibility—difficult, but immensely meaningful. This is to acquire the courage to innovate and experiment without sacrificing the core ideals of higher education. Only then is it possible for us to create theoretical activists or activist theoreticians (not anti-philosophical 'skilled resources'), and creative human agents (not passive role-performers) who would eventually realize the need to integrate vocational and educational aims into a 'liberal vocationalism' which, as Barnett would have argued, aims at both self-enlightenment and societal enlightenment (Ibid: 81). Indian universities, as I am trying to argue, need such an innovative spirit. Unless we offer better alternatives, how can we succeed in fighting the evils of commodification of education?

Choosing motivated students

Whether or not one chooses to join a college/university should depend on one's *swadharma*: one's temperament, inclination and aptitude. That is why, it is desirable that only those who are willing to bear and accept the demands of higher education—intellectual/moral eagerness to explore the ever-expanding frontiers of knowledge, and mental qualities like perseverance, patience and willingness to see beyond the logic of immediate utility—should join colleges and universities as young learners. Quite often, as I have already indicated in earlier chapters, schools fail to arouse this sense of freedom and choice. Instead, because of the societal and peer pressure, students find themselves obsessed with the diploma disease. Is it because we continue to privilege the mental/intellectual over the physical/manual, and some sort of prestige is still associated with a college/university degree, despite its devaluation in recent times? Or, is it because we have not yet been able to create sufficient centres and institutes to attract those who have the aptitude for diverse occupations ranging from tailoring to horticulture? Whatever be the reason, the fact is that Indian colleges/universities are terribly overcrowded. I do admit that the spirit of democratization demands more and more aspirants joining the domain of higher learning. I also admit that we need more colleges/universities to fulfil these growing aspirations. However, as I am arguing, democratization does by no means mean trivialization of higher education; instead, it means creating situations that enable the truly motivated ones to our colleges/universities. Otherwise, the result would be disastrous, and we would find amidst ourselves only demotivated students. Anyone who has taught in a college/university knows how depressing it is to teach Plato and Marx, or Milton and Tagore to a group of students who are by no means inclined to a deeper and fundamental philosophical quest, and instead, demand something else: more tangible and more worldly. As a result, young minds and their possibilities get destroyed. One who could have become an extraordinarily creative farmer destroys three valuable years while attending classes on Karl Popper's *Conjectures and Refutations*. Or, imagine what happens when one who is potentially a good tailor is sent to a lecture hall in which the professor delivers a lecture on quantum mechanics!

> I have no problem with weak students. What, however, shocks me is the presence of indifferent ones. They simply refuse to respond...It was a class of 200 students. One day I was teaching the relevance of 'biographical' approach in sociology. Could you believe that none knew the meaning of biography?

As a young teacher of a reputed undergraduate college in Darjeeling narrated his anguish, I could feel the crisis. Demotivation destroys the very rhythm of learning. A solution can emerge only if a thousand flowers are allowed to bloom, and people get an opportunity to find the vocations they are inclined to. Let, as visionaries like Ruskin and Gandhi wanted, a society evolve in which there is dignity of labour, and a professor and a tailor occupy their legitimate space without any sense of extra pride or undue stigmatization. Only then is it possible for our universities to find students who are truly inclined to the ideals of higher education, and pursue it for its joy, and the challenges it provides, but not for a faulty notion of social recognition, or for passing time.

Once we find truly motivated students it becomes easier to overcome the much talked about pathology: discontent and meaninglessness among students leading to widespread campus violence. It is really sad that this violence has crossed all limits. It is, therefore, not surprising that a distinguished educationist has to plead for a 'separate police cadre to deal with students' (Singh 1989: 227). Not solely that. This violence often acquires a political character, and as a result, the very idea of students' politics has begun to repel vice chancellors and policy makers. At this juncture, an ethical question confronts us. None can deny that campus politics is becoming terribly ugly. Money and muscle power, lumpenism and absence of ideals and values tend to characterize this politics. Seldom is it possible to come across a registrar or a vice chancellor who has not been *gheraoed,* and against whom slogans (and quite often nasty slogans) have not been raised. The sanctity of the teacher-taught relationship seems to be disappearing. Instead, what prevails is an environment filled with fear, mistrust and suspicion. But then, it has to be realized, there is no instant administrative/bureaucratic solution. Essentially, it requires deeper changes in the very culture of learning. Without a meaningful curriculum and motivated students, as I am trying to argue, it would not be possible to come forward with enduring solutions. It is in this sense that I would argue that politics as such need not be feared and perceived as some sort of taboo (in fact, as history has taught us, our universities, since the early days of decolonization, have been generating radical ideas and voices of dissent leading to socio-political movements). It should not be forgotten that when a creative/critical culture of learning prevails, politics itself becomes a great source of learning. Training in politics is, after all, a mode of understanding the dynamics of power in human society: how we manage our affairs, distribute our resources, define development and progress, and make comprehensive plans for the nation. These are issues involving conflicting interests and diverse ideological perspectives. And politics—if practised meaningfully—gives us the much required sensitivity to make our presence felt in such a grand project. When it is such an important component of human life, how can we deprive students of having an engagement with it?

In fact, the idea of an apolitical campus in which students are concerned only with their grades and careers is terrifying. It is like promoting selfishness, and nurturing a mindset that dissociates itself from all sorts of collective concerns. And this indifference gets further legitimated because politics itself, as any careful observer of Indian social reality would admit, has become terribly dirty that hardly reminds one of what Gramsci or Gandhi visualized. Yet, the answer to immoral/violent politics is not depoliticization, but an alternative politics which itself is an exercise in critical pedagogy. I feel tempted to cite the example of the Jawaharlal Nehru University: the way its students have created and protected a culture of alternative politics. It is not that JNU politics is free from all aberrations; it is possible to find the traces of casteism, regionalism, crude Machiavellianism and even occasional violence. Yet, what distinguishes this politics is its creativity: the way students themselves conduct their own elections, call public meetings, organize debates and seminars, write posters and theoretically enriched pamphlets, relate the local to the global, and discuss issues ranging from development and displacement to American imperialism and Gulf War. It is indeed difficult to distinguish the critical pedagogy prevalent in the university from this politics which, I believe, can become a model for other universities to follow. In order to demonstrate the intensity of ideological debate in which JNU students participate, let me quote from a pamphlet written by a radical group on the phenomenon called *Nandigarm*:

> ...At Delhi, one could see a visibly angry, shivering CPM secretary Prakash Karat, insisting that it is the Maoists who are responsible for the spiralling of violence in Nandigram. Had it not been for the Maoists, things could have been settled in an amicable manner. What was the issue actually was never of his concern. So for the CPM secretary and his Chief Minister it was justified to do whatever at one's disposal—be it shooting with SLRs and AK-47s at peaceful demonstrations by trained CPM goons, burning down houses of the people of Nandigram,

> mass rape of women, maiming the people—when you are pitted against the Maoists. The people cannot or should not stand with the Maoists. Nor can the Maoists talk about or support the genuine causes of the toiling masses. Any issue becomes a non issue when the Maoists raise it. Nandigram, Special Economic Zones, Displacement, Destitution, Destruction, Death—everything becomes a non issue because the Maoists are raising it.[15]

It is just an illustration. There are voices and counter-voices. The debate goes on. What else is a university if its students do not become, to use Amartya Sen's words, sufficiently 'argumentative'?

In search of creative teachers

No centre for higher learning can unfold its potential without dedicated and energetic teachers. It is, however, unfortunate that not many teachers can be said to have a very positive self-esteem. An important reason for this wounded consciousness is that as a society we have not yet been able to learn to respect the vocation of teaching, and keep its spirit alive. We live amidst the hierarchy of professions, and in terms of all that matters, be it social recognition or material reward, teachers, as many believe, exist nowhere compared to, say, management executives, media professionals, doctors, engineers and civil servants. Moreover, as every insider knows, there are many in the vocation itself who are not truly inclined to its calling. The very purpose of teaching—exploring new ideas, communicating with the younger generation, and willingness to remain perpetually fresh and alert—does not seem to have much appeal to them. Teaching, for them, becomes merely a routine. This further degrades the vocation.

Things must change. We must try to find creative and motivated teachers. Yes, it goes without saying, teachers—if we want them to give their best—need to be given their due. Their material conditions (in terms of salary, research/field trip grants, contingency expenses, medical and housing facilities) must improve substantially. It is also important to appoint more teachers, and reduce the heavy load of work which often goes against creativity. Imagine a situation in which a teacher delivers a lecture before 150 undergraduate students. Or, think of a teacher who has to deliver five lectures every day! Where is, then, the possibility of a meaningful teacher-taught relationship? Yes, a reasonably improved infrastructure, needless to add, is conducive to good teaching. But then, it must be realized that there is no substitute for inner calling. Unless one loves the very ethos of teaching and celebrates its creative restlessness, no amount of material reward can alter the situation. The moot question is: how do we find and recruit such motivated teachers?

Let us look at the prevalent process of recruitment of college/university teachers. After the advertisement for the specified position, candidates apply. And then the shortlisted candidates (shortlisting is often done mechanically, and on the basis of the necessary qualifications alone) are called for the interview. A selection committee consisting of the head of the institute and a couple of subject experts is constituted to interview the candidates. It all depends on the number of candidates and the mood of the selection committee—interview can last for only five minutes or even forty minutes. And eventually the selection committee gives its final judgment. This process of elimination and selection, I would argue, is inherently problematic. Anyone who has experienced it (either as a candidate or as a member of the selection committee) knows that it has two major shortcomings. First, interview as an exercise of asymmetrical power relations (experts ask and interrogate; there is no possibility of a dialogue in which even candidates can open up, and raise counter-questions) often causes excessive psychic pressure, and makes it difficult for a candidate to give her best. Habermas would have characterized it as a 'broken/distorted communication'. Second, experts, it would not be entirely wrong to say, often celebrate this power; they do not mind reducing the entire exercise into a quiz contest. Not much space is given to the candidate to elaborate, explain, argue, and present a complex phenomenon with all its ambiguities. Instead, to take a real example from sociology, a candidate may be asked to provide readymade answers to the following:

1. In which year did Malinowski conduct his field study among Trobriand Islanders?
2. Define society. Is it a process? Or is it a structure?
3. Mention the 'pattern variables' Talcott Parsons talked about.

If at that unnatural moment one cannot remember the exact date of Malinowski's field work, or if one's perception of society does not coincide with the way a standard textbook or the Oxford dictionary of sociology defines it, or if one does not feel very comfortable with Talcott Parsons, one is declared 'bad'—not fit for teaching! That is the irony. No attempt is being made to understand what the candidate knows, her depth of knowledge, and overall sociological imagination. It is quite possible that the candidate who has been eliminated knows pretty well how Malinowski's *Sex and Repression in a Savage Society* refuted Sigmund Freud's universal theories of the Oedipus Complex, or how Durkheim, Weber and Marx enriched our understanding of the creative and dialectical interplay of structure and agency in human society, or how Talcott Parsons' functionalist preoccupation with 'order' and 'system' was criticized by many critical sociologists. But then, where is the time or, for that matter, inclination for engaging in a meaningful dialogue with the candidate?

One way of overcoming this limitation, I believe, is to make the process of recruitment more transparent, democratic and effective. Let the shortlisted candidates (and shortlisting should not be done mechanically; apart from the necessary qualifications, emphasis should also be put on the other desirable qualities) be invited to the concerned department to deliver a lecture on any theme of their own choice. Let students, teachers and selection committee members participate in the discussion, and take an active part in making the second round of shortlisting on the basis of their performance: their communicative skills, their ability to persuade the audience, their analytical capacity and their depth of knowledge. And finally, let the selection committee engage in an elaborated conversation with them, and give its final judgment. Even though it is a relatively time-consuming process, it would lead to better results. Moreover, once teachers are appointed, we need to evolve a system of feedback and evaluation by students which would further enable them to keep their creative zeal alive. Good teachers, it should not be forgotten, create a good university, and consolidate its moral foundation.

VII
MERIT AS A QUALITY OF BEING

This discussion would, however, remain incomplete unless we look at yet another ethical question confronting us: does excellence in higher education necessarily mean promotion of meritocracy and thereby negation of social justice and equality? None would dispute the fact that excellence is what a university should strive for—excellence in research, in teaching, and in academic performance of students. At the same time, it is equally important for a university to remain inclusive and accommodative, and take a leading role in reducing social disparities. Is it possible to reconcile these two ideals: excellence and equality? Indian universities, needless to add, are experiencing this challenge rather sharply, and it has generated a series of complex issues relating to the very purpose of higher education.

To begin with, let us historicize the problem. We live in a society that continues to retain the legacy of caste hierarchy and social exclusion. But then, it is also a society that passed through a profound struggle for decolonization, and embraced an egalitarian project of nation-making. From diverse forms of social reform projects to the historic struggle that luminaries like Gandhi and Ambedkar launched in their own respective styles—it was becoming increasingly clear that as a new nation we would be required to abolish a system based on hierarchy, ascriptive status, purity and pollution, and social and cultural exclusion. Furthermore, with the process of democratization and growing assertion of the hitherto marginalized groups, a new consciousness has begun to emerge that strives for equity and justice. As a matter of fact, the demand for equality of opportunity and access to education has become an integral component of this new assertion. It is in this historic context that the Constitutional provision of protective discrimination or reservation begins to make sense. Its basic philosophy is simple and clear. In order to create a truly equal society, we need to give extra benefit to those who, without any fault their own, have been lagging behind; this encouragement, it is believed, would enable them to overcome the historic burden of marginalization, and become truly equal citizens of a regenerated nation.

Against this background, let us look at the state of our universities. As I have already discussed, our universities, barring exceptions, are not really excellent centres of teaching and research. But at the same time, our universities, it must be acknowledged, have not escaped from the societal role: satisfying the aspirations of the marginalized and oppressed sections of society. None can deny that, because of the policy of protective discrimination, students from the hitherto marginalized communities are joining the domain of higher education, and altering their life-projects. Even though an absolutely egalitarian society remains a distant dream, some significant changes are taking place in the culture of the university. Let me speak of some of these positive changes. First, we see the emergence of *heterogeneity* which, I believe, has immense pedagogic significance. For example, each time I come to the class, I realize that I have to communicate with a wide spectrum of students having diverse socio-economic backgrounds, and different levels of oral/written skills. This poses a serious challenge, and inspires me to continually reflect on my pedagogy—the way I deliver my lecture, the examples I cite, the jokes I crack, the assignments I prepare—so that neither English-speaking/metropolitan students, nor those coming from the peripheries of Jharkhand and Orissa get alienated and marginalized in the class. In this process an attempt is being made to create an open/dialogic/inclusive culture in the classroom. Possibly stereotypes are broken, and students from diverse backgrounds begin to interact. This leads to the fusion of horizons. I am not suggesting that this is an easy and smooth process. Social prejudices and stereotypes do not die easily. Quite often, students belonging to the similar socio-economic background constitute their own sub-groups, and seek to retain a distance from the rest. Nevertheless, it is only in a heterogeneous setting that emancipatory possibilities of cross-cultural interaction can arise. For example, a Dalit boy and a forward caste/metropolitan girl can be asked to be part of the same team, work together, and complete a project. Without providing such challenges, as I have learned from my own experience, I could not have reflected on the implications of my pedagogy, and then possibly I could have remained contented only with the academic charm of 'meritocracy', and its implicit elitism.

Second, in this very process I witness and experience our new role, our contributions to the process of transformation that students, particularly from the margins and peripheries, are undergoing. Yes, universities give them hope, enable them to unfold their potential, and make a difference. Let me narrate the experience of one such student:

> I am from Champaran—from a remote village. I joined Jawaharlal Nehru University in 2003. Initially, there were many problems. My English was terribly bad. I could not express myself in the class. Nor could I write well. But I didn't give up. I tried. And eventually things began to change. I am now relatively more comfortable. I am learning continuously. ... Indeed, I am fortunate to be part of this university. It has changed me a lot. It has given me a new direction of thinking: a spirit of understanding, and above all a ray of hope.[16]

Indeed, as a teacher it fills my mind with joy when I see this process of transformation closely and intimately: the way they overcome their initial hesitation, conquer obstacles, acquire confidence, complete their education, and become teachers, civil servants, media professionals and innovative social activists.

Third, this entire process, I believe, has its positive impact on the production of knowledge. For example, these days it is difficult to think of a university in which *Dalit studies* are not gaining legitimacy; new questions are raised—questions relating to the curriculum, and methods of teaching and research. Moreover, a new sensitivity emerges that leads to a creative research in sociology, politics and literature. For example, today we are told how even some of the finest pieces of literature (even the creations of a literary figure like Premchand) have not been able to capture the Dalit mind; how the dominant/mainstream sociology has been written from the perspectives of the forward caste intelligentsia (a leading political sociologist is now asserting why he is not a 'Hindu'); and how even the Marxists are not qualitatively different from a 'bunch of Brahmins'! Although as a teacher/researcher, I need not necessarily agree with all these findings, the fact is that the plurality of perspectives, viewpoints and ideologies has indeed contributed to the intellectual and moral growth of the university. Possibly it democratizes our university when we find scholars and researchers seeing beyond Gandhi, Tagore and Nehru, and, instead, engaging with Phule, Periyar and Ambedkar.

These positive consequences notwithstanding, there are serious questions regarding the entire issue which, I believe, need to be responded to with an open mind. For example, it is often debated whether the principle of protective discrimination/reservation can really be reconciled with the ideal of higher education, i.e. promoting excellence in teaching and research. Beteille, for example, has expressed this anxiety rather sharply:

> Every time a candidate of superior academic merit is passed over to make place for one who is less than his academic equal, some damage is done to the foundations on which the university stands. It is not clear that the damage becomes smaller when justification for such action is sought in the need for creating parity between castes. ...It cannot distribute its rewards—whether examination grades, or scholarships or faculty appointments—on the basis of quotas determined by political bargains. Above all, universities should not allow themselves to become hunting grounds for leaders of castes and communities negotiating for shares in their rewards for their own constituencies, irrespective of merit (Beteille 1988: 141-42).

This is a serious point which deserves attention. And that is why, at this juncture it is important to reflect on the notion of academic merit itself, or the qualities which are thought to be valuable and necessary for excelling in the domain of higher education. There are primary three components of this much-desired merit. First, what one needs is a *spirit of learning*: intellectual zeal and enthusiasm, analytical mind, familiarity with basic foundations, and willingness to explore the new horizon of knowledge. Second, one needs a specific *mental state*: patience, perseverance, and above all, ability to appreciate a mode of life that involves continual engagement with new ideas, even non-utilitarian ideas. And third, one also needs some sort of *cultural capital*—say, reasonable knowledge in English, exposure to cultural/intellectual debates, and a style of writing (possibly this is more important in liberal arts, humanities and social sciences)—that enables one to move from the concrete to the abstract. Anyone who has lived in a university—I mean a university that seeks to promote serious teaching and research—knows that those who are endowed with these qualities are generally called 'meritorious', and they perform reasonably well.

No caste/class, we all realize, is inherently superior, and gifted with these qualities. Essentially, life-chances, social experiences and cultural environment play an important role in shaping the evolution of these attributes in one's biography. It is, of course, true that because of the historic burden of marginalization it becomes exceedingly difficult for the children of the oppressed castes to get an opportunity to acquire these qualities. Likewise, poverty, regional deprivation and gender discrimination further add to these obstacles.

This, however, does not mean that the children from the relatively privileged classes are naturally endowed with these qualities. It is, of course, true that because of their family traditions (particularly, if the parents are 'culturally sensitive') they may acquire the necessary *cultural capital* quite early—say, developing a distinctive taste for good books, classical music, abstract painting and radical theatre. However, these qualities would wither away if they are not sustained and developed through constant practices. That is why, if given an opportunity, even the children of the marginalized sections of society can overcome their initial difficulties, and acquire and retain these attributes. Essentially, what we regard as 'merit' has to be perpetually nurtured and cultivated, and in our times schools have to play an important role in sharpening these qualities. That is why, in a hierarchical society like ours, special measures have to be taken (by the welfare state as well as the larger society) so that all children, irrespective of caste, class and gender, can get good quality school education, and find an opportunity to excel in life. It is sad that as a nation we have not yet been able to implement what the Kothari Commission regarded as a *common school system*: a system which wanted to overcome all sorts of hierarchies and dualities like 'the minority of private, fee-charging, better schools meeting the needs of the upper classes', vs. 'the vast bulk of free, publicly maintained, but poor schools being utilized by the rest', and to give quality education to all. If we sincerely strive for equality, there is, in fact, no other way. Moreover, as it has been repeatedly asserted by the radical left, it is important to initiate structural changes for bringing about economic opportunities for the downtrodden. It is also desirable to retain the spirit of cultural transformation so that all that is associated with a caste-based patriarchal social order withers away. In the absence of these sustained efforts at the level of school education as well as economic and cultural fronts, protective discrimination or reservation alone is not adequate. Instead, it is bound to have its moments of tension, anxiety and apprehension. Anyone who has taught in a university , wrote Beteille, 'knows how little he can do to alter the mental habits of students who have passed their teens, and how hard it is at that age to raise the ill-equipped student to even the level of the average' (Ibid: 14).

I see a point in Beteille's concern. As teachers we all have found students who refuse to grow, who find themselves strangers in an academic environment. They tend to develop all sorts of complexes. And it becomes exceedingly difficult for a teacher to alter this asymmetry in the classroom. Yet, I would argue that even under these unfavourable circumstances, universities have to play an active role, include those who are not as 'meritorious' as we otherwise want our students to be, and initiate special measures (extra classes/remedial programmes) so that they can gain confidence, rise up, and unfold their potential. It is, however, possible if they show their willingness and sincerity. It is sad that, at times, some of them begin to see it only as a 'right'; they forget that this right can become truly enabling only if it is endowed with responsibilities. As a result, they refuse to grow. Reservation becomes a vested interest. And in a political culture that refuses to see beyond reservation, how often we hear only of 'rights', but not motivation, inner calling, responsibility and hard work. Yet, as I have learned from my own experiences, there are students who intend to evolve and grow. As teachers we must engage with them in the process of their transformation.

It is a difficult but not an impossible task. In my own teaching career I have often witnessed this process of wonderful transformation: how students who at one time did not have much confidence in English, and were not at all aware of the publications like *Economic and Political Weekly* and *Contributions to Indian Sociology* would eventually overcome their hesitation, begin to articulate, speak, write, and even debate with their privileged contemporaries. Not solely that. Quite often, these students have another kind of *capital* which we must learn to value, particularly in the sphere of social sciences and humanities. This capital stems from the experiences they have gained through their sufferings, the knowledge they have acquired through their everyday engagement with caste hierarchy, village politics and agrarian conflict. They may not have the academic language to articulate it. But then, if in a dialogic environment they are listened to with care and concern, it would benefit the professor, and more particularly the privileged students who may have read Marx, but may not have ever lived in a village; who may have mastered the art of using appropriate sociological idioms and concepts, but may not be able to initiate a simple conversation with a landless peasant! I would, therefore, argue that in the name of 'meritocracy' a university should not take up an elitist position. Because a university needs to engage itself—and with absolute concern and empathy—with the struggles taking place in the larger society. What else is merit if it does not inspire one to share the sufferings of others, and relate to collective welfare? Merit is not just about publications, books and academic awards. Merit is also a quality of being: an experience of oneness, and willingness to share.

There is yet another problem. Those who are getting the benefits of reservation often acquire *stigmatized* identities. It is like marking them perpetually, and generating a stereotype: 'Here is a group not adequately meritorious, and hence destroying the quality of higher education'. This stigma is a sort of existential anguish, and students from the oppressed castes continue to experience this marginalization, even when they are attending classes, writing exams, and doing reasonably well (whereas it is possible to come across students from the privileged classes escaping their responsibilities as students/ researchers). This stigma has acquired added intensity in recent times because in almost every Indian university we find a significant section of students—primarily from the privileged classes and forward castes—who oppose, and oppose vehemently, the policy of reservation. Yes, it is possible to see the traces of casteism and elitism in their gestures—in the very symbolism of the recent upsurge of 'anti-quota movements'. But then, it should not be forgotten, they are also making a point which deserves attention. After all, they too are anxious, and their insecurity is not unreal; it is rooted in a ruthlessly aggressive competitive culture in which, because of scarcity of opportunities, everybody—not excluding forward caste students—lives with terrible survival anxiety. Moreover, they are not entirely wrong in arguing that we have to seriously rethink the policy of giving reservation to those who, despite their lower caste origin, are privileged: economically, politically or otherwise. Likewise, even some forward caste students, because of poverty or other forms of deprivation, may require reservation. Can a university remain altogether indifferent to these concerns? The fact is that our universities need to see beyond the paradigm of 'identity politics', and move towards a more unified struggle for collective welfare.

Indeed, our universities are facing the dilemma: a sort of moral ambiguity. We must argue that reservation alone would not succeed in creating an egalitarian society. We must remind the political class that without substantial democratization of society, distribution of material resources, and availability of quality school education to all, reservation in universities would continue to cause acute tension and anxiety. Yet, as I have already suggested, this does by no means mean that by delegating the entire responsibility to the political class, we should retreat into our small world of excellence. We too need to open up, create consciousness, and work with those who, even if not 'meritorious', have hidden potential. What else is a university if it refuses to engage with these moral experiments?

NOTES

1. In a way, the heroic notion of science (science is 'objective', 'value-neutral' and 'apolitical') has been interrogated by many philosophers of science. From Popper to Kuhn to Feyerabend—we now know the vulnerability of science. Furthermore, with postmodern celebration of differences (against meta narratives Lyotard posits a discourse of multiple horizons, the play of language games, and the terrain of micro politics), the ideal of science as the most privileged truth gets debunked.
2. As told by a professor of education from JNU.
3. As told by a professor of Portuguese language and literature from JNU.
4. As told by a professor of biotechnology from JNU.
5. From a newspaper report: *Ph.Ds run dhaba* published in the New Delhi edition of the *The Hindustan Times* (4.12.2001).
6. As told by a professor of economics of education from JNU.
7. As told by a professor of Portuguese language and literature from JNU.
8. As told by a professor of Arabic language and literature from JNU.
9. As told by a professor of economics from Delhi University.
10. The report was prepared by two leading industrialists—Mukesh Ambani and Kumarmangalam Birla. And it was presented before the nation on April 24, 2000.
11. From a newspaper report: *Head to Manipal for professional courses* published in the New Delhi Edition of *The Hindustan Times* (21.05.2008).
12. Interestingly, Amity University—a leading private university—proudly declares 'Over 2000 Amity students have got on-campus

placements this year. Also, over 500 students have been placed even one year before graduating'. And then, in its admission notice for Post-Graduate Programmes it declares the list of courses and programmes to be offered. Not surprisingly, the courses are heavily market-oriented. The following sample indicates the trend:

M.Tech-Biotechnology; Master of Film and TV Production; M.Sc.-Interior Design; MBA-Hospitality Management; PG Dip. in Insurance Management; PG Dip. in NGO Management; M.A.-Tourism Administration.

For further details, see the ad published in the New Delhi edition of *The Hindustan Times* (20.01.2008).

13. Champion guide books are quite popular among undergraduate students of the University of Delhi.
14. From her written response to my enquiry.
15. From a pamphlet entitled *Nandigram: The Brutal Force of Social Fascist CPM* issued by the JNU Unit of DSU on November 22, 2007.
16. From his written response to my enquiry.

Conclusion

HOPE AMIDST DESPAIR: THE BEAUTY OF TEACHING

This book, readers must have already felt, is a protest against a system of learning that gets increasingly dissociated from finer ethical issues, and reduces itself into a mere technical skill or a marketable commodity. But it is also about hope, about a new possibility that with a critical/reflexive pedagogy we can restore ethical/moral issues in the domain of education, and thereby contribute to the making of a just/egalitarian/sensitive society.

One may ask: can this hope be sustained? As a matter of fact, hope and anxiety; hidden possibility and practical constraint—there seems no escape from this ongoing dialectic. And there are moments when despair and cynicism envelop our consciousness, and we tend to think that a just society is an impossible project, and there can be no relief from aggression, competitiveness and narcissism. In our times, it would not be wrong to say, there are many who often experience this despair. Apparently, this looks paradoxical, because our age is otherwise being characterized by a spirit of dynamism: constant change and movement towards new ventures!

Let us understand this dialectic. We all know that what social scientists regard as a project of modernity is centred on a grand hope: it is possible to create a better world—a democratic world with freedom and self-dignity; equality of opportunity and justice. In fact, scientific reasoning and technological development, as the narrative of hope indicates, would take us to this new world free from poverty and physical suffering, medieval orthodoxy and tyranny of religious institutions. This hope, needless to add, gave immense momentum to the world, and there was massive transformation. Liberal democracy, human rights and techno-economic development—all these processes, many would argue, enabled us to live longer, generate surplus, experience freedom , and lead a comfortable life with sufficient leisure and entertainment. But then, this hope, it seems, cannot always be sustained. In this post-Enlightenment era, we are now talking more about spectacular violence manifesting itself in all sorts of hyper-technological war and terrorist violence; poverty amidst vulgar affluence; religious fundamentalism and identity politics as another side of asymmetrical globalization; and above all, innumerable risks emerging out of global warming and environmental damage caused by ruthless techno-economic development. Moreover, doubts are being raised about the efficacy of some of the revolutionary ideals that once inspired people to dream of a better world. Take, for instance, the fate of Marxism. The degeneration of Soviet socialism into a state-centric tyranny, and eventually the collapse of the Soviet Union; the process through which advanced capitalism with its expanding service sector and a high standard of living has drastically altered the classical notion of the 'revolutionary' working class; and above all, the way the ethos of global capitalism with its culture industry, consumerism and simulation has conquered all boundaries—everything seems to indicate that we are now living in a world in which not revolutionary ideals, but social Darwinism reigns supreme. In such a scenario, critical theorists saw 'instrumental rationality', Foucault found 'surveillance'; and for postmodernists, history is dead, and no grand narrative of progress is feasible any more. Where is then the hope that we can create a better world, and make a new beginning? The way Eric Hobsbawm captured this dialectic deserves our attention:

> We live in a world captured, uprooted and transformed by the titanic economic and techno-scientific process of the development of capitalism, which has dominated the past two or three centuries. We know, or at least it is reasonable to suppose, that it cannot go on *ad infinitum*. The future cannot

> be a continuation of the past, and there are signs, both externally, and, as it were, internally, that we have reached a point of historic crisis. The forces generated by the techno-scientific economy are now great enough to destroy the environment, that is to say, the material foundations human life. The structures of human societies themselves, including even some of the social foundations of the capitalist economy, are on the point of being destroyed by the erosion of what we have inherited from the human past. Our world risks both explosion and implosion. It must change.... We do not know where we are going. We only know that history has brought us to this point. ... If humanity is to have a recognizable future, it cannot be by prolonging the past or the present. If we try to build the third millennium on that basis, we shall fail. And the price of failure, that is to say, the alternative to a changed society is darkness (Hobsbawm 1996 : 584-85).

Indeed, if we do not change ourselves, the future, as the celebrated historian argues, is bleak. But do we have the optimism for initiating the much deserved change? Even when we look at contemporary India, we see a similar dialectic. True, the spirit of decolonization was filled with a grand hope that new India would emerge; from Swami Vivekananda's 'practical Vedanta' to Mohandas Karamchand Gandhi's 'experiments' with politics and religion—new India, it was believed, would find her inspiration to stand up, and get herself free from fatalism and stagnation, or hierarchy and oppression. 'India', as Jawaharlal Nehru put it, 'will find herself again when freedom opens out new horizons, and the future will then fascinate her more than the immediate past of frustration and humiliation' (Nehru 1983: 564). Not solely that. 'India', Nehru added, 'will go forward with confidence, rooted in herself, and yet eager to learn from others and cooperate with them' (Ibid: 564). This grand hope, however, got shattered. Partition came as a severe blow to the ethos of universalism, cosmopolitanism and cultural syncretism. Gandhi's assassination was yet another indicator: it was the death of an experiment, death of a vision: a vision that with spiritualized politics, decentralization of power, an economy based on genuine human needs rather than greed, and above all, a symmetrical relationship with nature, new India would experience real *swaraj*, and evolve an alternative to violent and ruthless techno-capitalism. Yes, like all great visions, it too looked utopian; but then, a society that devalues Utopias begins to degenerate. Even the early euphoria of nation-making (through 'scientific temper', secularism and state-initiated developmental projects) that charismatic Nehru symbolized seems to have withered away. At times, one tends to feel that fragmentation and regionalism, inequality and violence, communalism and identity politics, and corruption and selfishness characterize our times. It is, of course, true that India did progress. None could deny its techno-economic structure, its reasonable success with parliamentary democracy, and its achievements in science, art and literature. However, this progress, many would fear, is so uneven that it cannot generate a sense of collectivity, a spirit of togetherness. Yes, at one level, particularly because of the neo-liberal agenda that India has been pursuing since the 1990s, there is immense dynamism which we see in the accelerating growth rate, in the vitality of the share market, and in the expansion of the middle class. Not surprisingly, we live amidst all sorts of urban mythologies that promise diverse packages of 'good life'. Take one such mythology:

> You wished it, we created it. A home just minutes from Delhi but away from the maddening crowd. Where you can stroll across to your office. Where you can rediscover yourself amidst greenery, lakes, trails and nature parks. Where you can open your windows and greet the clouds each morning. Where your children can take their time to grow. Come, be a part of the world that fulfils all your wishes and then let you wish for more.[1]

Incidentally, the ad of this gorgeous housing project has been titled 'Our wishes have been fulfilled. So can be yours!' And that is precisely the paradox. Not everyone's wishes can be fulfilled in this way. While all these mythologies propagated through credit card economy, real estate business, tourism packages and shopping malls seek to promise a new/mythical world for the affluent; poverty, hunger, starvation death, displacement, homelessness, unemployment, and much talked-about Naxalite upsurge make us feel that despair is all around. Cynicism, needless to add, enters deep into our minds. That is why, the question: how can we dare to hope, speak of ethics, think of a better world, and plead for a creative and radical pedagogy?

Yet, as I wish to argue, what keeps us alive is our ability to dissent, and evolve zones of possibilities. It is in this sense that life is a continual journey: a movement towards light amidst darkness or, as Faiz Ahmed Faiz would have felt, life is a 'harvest of hopes': a belief that

some day a ripe harvest shall be ours.
Till that day, we must plough the sands.[2]

No wonder, irrespective of the all-pervasive despair, we continue to find creative groups, people with zeal and optimism, or, to use the language of sociology, people endowed with agency. That is why, socio-political movements take place, experiments are being made, new possibilities emerge, and there is a quest for a spiritually elevated, ecologically sensitive, egalitarian social order. It is, therefore, not surprising that, despite commodification and marketization of education, we find amongst ourselves alternative schools, creative educationists, and silent/dedicated teachers who seek to make a difference, and convey a message that it is possible to tap the potential of critical and reflexive pedagogy, and contribute to the making of a just society.

I too am rooted in this human situation. Even when I am aware that obstacles are enormous, I realize that possibilities are still alive. That is why, in this book an attempt has been made to examine how we can work in the domain of education, restore its moral significance, and move towards a just society. The visualization of this possibility, I wish to emphasize, does not emerge out of void; it evolves because of our collective concerns and anxieties, and because of innumerable ventures, small or big, made by ordinary mortals like us to create a new foundation of education. And in this project, teachers, it is obvious, have to play a key role. This discussion would, therefore, remain incomplete without looking at the vocation of teaching. It is not my contention to suggest that a group of dedicated teachers alone can alter the educational scenario. The practice of education, sociology has taught to, is organically related to the larger social structure: its polity, economy and culture. A radical change in the domain of education is not possible without structural changes. But then, no revolution is possible without small changes you and I make in our respective domains of work. A school, a university, a classroom—every site is, therefore, important, and good teachers endowed with a vision can at least initiate the process of socio-cultural transformation we are talking about.

We are, however, living at a time when new realities have begun to interrogate the relevance and significance of the teaching community itself. Are teachers as human agents relevant any more in a world that lives in abundance, celebrates instantaneity, and privileges technological solutions? For instance, radical innovations in the domain of information technology—easy availability of e-mail and the Internet—are questioning the very relevance of a physical site called the classroom in which teachers and students engage in a direct face-to-face communication. Furthermore, with open schools and distant education the teacher as an embodiment of wisdom is fast disappearing. Photocopies, open school/university learning material, and the Internet, it may be argued, reduce the significance of the teacher. While these changes arouse concern and anxiety, the fact remains that the relevance of the human agency of the teacher can by no means be negated. There are two reasons. First, knowledge is not just information, and even if every learner has an access to the Internet, she requires the guidance of a teacher to find a way out from this jungle of information, to process and assimilate, to derive a meaning, and to theorize and conceptualize. Technology, no matter how sophisticated and refined, cannot replace the role of teachers—a job that requires human touch and a spirit of continual dialogue and reflection. Second, as we are repeatedly arguing, education is not just about academic cognition; it is also about a sense of beauty and justice. Can technology alone accomplish this aesthetic/spiritual function of education? Acquiring this sensitivity requires a real and alive human presence: when we experience the wonder of charisma, and see someone unfolding her creativity, acting like a catalyst, inspiring and encouraging us to realize our innate possibilities. In a way this need or quest is very real, and learning remains utterly inadequate and incomplete in an anonymous/impersonal world. That is why, the relevance of teachers as embodied beings filled with knowledge and wisdom can by no means be negated.

A vocation of this kind, needless to add, is immensely demanding. Teaching invariably implies grand ideals. In fact, in a civilization like ours one ideal that has elevated this vocation is that of a *guru*: a charismatic spiritual leader radiating knowledge and wisdom, and showing the learner the road to the Absolute and the Eternal. Indeed, some of the finest *Upanishads* reveal this grand ideal: how, for instance, Yagnavalkya initiated a profound debate on the nature of the Self, and illuminated us about true knowledge (*vidya*): the ultimate reality which is beyond all sorts of dualities and forms. This quest, we were repeatedly reminded, would require single-minded devotion, calmness, clarity, and above all, purification of the mind. In this ideal a teacher becomes not just an instructor or a knowledgeable man; she/he becomes a finest philosopher or a great friend who illuminates, awakens, overcomes ignorance, and takes us 'from darkness to light'. Possibly a teacher as a friend-philosopher-guide is reflected rather strikingly in the *Bhagavadgita.* See the role of Krishna. Arjuna is his friend, his disciple, and Arjuna is in a terrible dilemma: whether or not to participate in the war that invariably implies the destruction, bloodshed and death of his own kinsmen. Krishna engages in a deep dialogue with Arjuna, makes him realize the deeper meaning of the war, and convinces him that he is required to participate in the war like a *karmayogi.* This entire discourse gives us some of the illuminating insights into the nature of the ultimate reality and the meaning of detachment and renunciation. Krishna is indeed a teacher who emerges at the time of crisis, generates calmness, and shows us the path to strive for. 'Destroyed is my delusion, and recognition has been gained by me through thy grace, O Acyuta (Krishna). I stand firm with my doubts dispelled. I shall act according to thy word' (XVIII. 73). Indeed, with Arjuna's realization, we see the greatness of a disciple to this guru! These ideals, I guess, have a deep-rooted impact on our notion of the vocation of teaching. A teacher is not just another paid employee. Nor is she merely an 'expert'. She is something more: someone to be trusted at the moment of crisis, someone who helps us discover paths to truth and wisdom Times, however, have changed. But these ideals continue to have their impact. No wonder, some of the finest educationists we found amongst ourselves in modern India—say, Rabindranath Tagore and Sri Aurbindo—did reveal this ideal in their own ways: seeing a teacher as a deeply humane and alive source of life-energy.

What is interesting to note is that such an ideal is not limited only to the Eastern spiritual discourse. Even in modern/secular times characterized by democratization, individuation and rationalization, the vocation of teaching continues to carry grand ideals which are no less demanding. Take, for instance, Emile Durkheim's celebrated text on moral education, and the way he narrated the role of the teacher in a modern society. For Durkheim, a teacher is no ordinary person; he is endowed with heavy responsibility; he represents the societal force which transcends the individual; it is his moral character, his firmness and determination, and his stability that would eventually convey a very important message to young learners: how to overcome egotism, internalize the collective ethos, and become truly social. And this authority, for Durkheim, does not emerge from the teacher's right to give punishment and reward. Indeed, it has a deeper moral significance. Durkheim stated it quite convincingly:

> This cannot come to him except from his innermost being. He must believe, not perhaps in himself or in the superior quality of his intelligence or will, but in his task and the greatness of that task. It is the priest's lofty conception of his mission that gives him the authority that so readily colours his language and bearing. For he speaks in the name of a God, who he feels in himself and to whom he feels himself much closer than the

> laymen in the crowds he addresses. So, the lay teacher can and should have something of this same feeling. He is also an instrument of a great moral reality which surpasses him and with which he communicates more directly than does the child, since it is through his intermediation that the child communicates with it. Just as the priest is the interpreter of God, he is the interpreter of the great moral ideas of his time and country (Durkheim 1961:155).

Again, if we think of Karl Mannheim—another great sociologist commenting on the crisis of the modern age—we see the reaffirmation of yet another beautiful ideal. A teacher, for Mannheim, cannot remain merely an instructor, someone who is concerned only with 'external rewards like marks, prizes and ranking'. Essentially, a teacher is one who ought to be concerned with the 'development of living'; his role is 'much broader and deeper which affects the personality of the pupil at all points and the relationship between the pupil and the teacher similarly' (Mannheim & Stewart 1962: 32).

See the power of this ideal. A teacher, it is thought, is also an emancipator—a revolutionary. Here is an unequal/asymmetrical world in which the 'wretched of the earth' are deprived of their voice, and inherit the 'culture of silence'. And in order to break this silence, interrogate this hierarchy and inequality, and to restore agency, reflexivity and criticality to people, we need new teachers who, as Paulo Freire imagined, would not be contented with 'banking education'; instead, they would work together with the learners, overcome all sorts of hierarchy and domination, and strive for an egalitarian ideal. It is only 'through dialogue', wrote Freire, 'the teacher-of-students and the students-of-teacher cease to exist, and a new term emerges: teacher-student with student-teacher' (Freire 1972: 53). Indeed, the 'inquiry method', as some educationists would argue (Postman and Weingartner 1971), is what gives a distinctive meaning to teaching. It prevents authoritarianism—the closure of minds. Instead, it allows ideas to evolve; it sees knowledge as a process; it arouses faith in each learner. Indeed, a teacher who follows the 'inquiry method'

> does not accept a single statement as an answer to a question. In fact, he has a persisting aversion to anyone, any syllabus, any text that offers the Right Answer. Not because answers and solutions are unwelcome—indeed, he is trying to help students be more efficient problem-solvers—but because he knows how often the Right Answer serves only to terminate further thought. He knows the power of pluralizing. He does not ask for the reason, but for the reasons. Not for the cause, but causes. Never the meaning, the meanings. He knows, too, the power of contingent thinking. He is the most 'It depends' learner in his class (Ibid: 44).

All these reflections indicate what I am trying to plead for: even in our times—modern/secular times—great ideals are associated with the vocation of teaching. A teacher is one who has something more than just cognitive/technical skill. She has a moral character, she is a source of energy and wisdom; she is someone to be trusted, and she inspires and motivates[3].

At this juncture another important question needs to be raised. Is there a qualitative difference between schoolteachers and college/university teachers? Schoolteachers interact with children who have just begun the trajectory of life. Schoolteachers are, therefore, not just teaching history or geography, mathematics or science; they are also moral guardians and role-models; their ethical/moral responsibility is tremendous. But then, unlike schoolteachers, college/university teachers are interacting with relatively mature adults whose personality structures have already been formed. And hence university teachers, it may be argued, need not have the added responsibility for 'character building'. Furthermore, the very nature of higher learning, it may be argued, is specialized; it requires the cultivation of 'expertized' knowledge. As the argument goes, a university teacher is, therefore, essentially a subject expert, a specialist, a researcher—not necessarily a 'friend/guide/philosopher'. While there is a point in this argument, it should, however, be remembered that this difference need not be overstated. Because, despite this difference, it is the ethos of teaching that unites them. Teaching itself, irrespective of the site in which it is taking place, means communication, an art of relatedness, and a bond involving life's delicate experiences: hope, expectation, fear, dilemma and anxiety. Anyone who has taught in a college/university knows that she cannot exist merely like a cold/detached/value-neutral subject 'expert'. Knowledge itself, no matter how specialized and technical, has its social implications that arouse political, moral and ethical questions. For instance, can a professor of biotechnology be altogether indifferent to its implications for social/cultural life? Or, for that matter, should a professor of physics close her eyes while seeing a concrete relationship between state and science, military and research? In other words, the social context in which knowledge is produced, disseminated and used is a major issue that teaching as a creative/critical practice must respond to for nurturing future citizens for a just society. Again, the relationship between the teacher and the taught is not like the relationship between the expert and the client. There are moments when both students and teachers experience diverse forms of crisis, and a strong bond helps them to cope with these difficult situations. It is all about concern and connectivity. And that is precisely its beauty; it is not a good idea to deprive the vocation of its charm.

A cynic may, however, argue that the beauty of teaching I am talking about is merely an empty ideal without any roots in reality. Yes, I do admit that if one looks at the prevalent reality one may get tempted to grow cynical. Teaching is now just another job—and that too without the minimal requirements that a reasonably decent standard of living demands. We are living at a time when the sanctity of the teacher-taught relationship is disappearing fast. Almost every day newspapers remind us of the prevalence of corporate punishment, campus violence, and all sorts of ugly experiences that seldom arouse faith in the vocation of teaching.[4]

In earlier chapters I have already indicated the possible reasons for this pathetic state of affairs. The prevalent hierarchy of professions privileges crude material or managerial/administrative power in the techno-corporate world, and thereby marginalizes the vocation of teaching as 'soft' and 'feminine' to be kept only for those who are not so 'bright', 'mobile' and 'ambitious'; the existing culture of learning which is characterized by poor infrastructure, bureaucratization, centralization, and exam-centric pedagogy further devalues the creative autonomy of teachers; and finally, a faulty mode of recruitment (which often gives importance to external qualifications like B.Ed. or Ph.D. degrees, rather than the inner calling, aptitude and inclination)—and that too in a social environment characterized by nepotism and corruption—makes it difficult to find sensitive and energetic teachers amongst us. It is, therefore, not surprising that many of them fail to realize the worth of their vacation. They lose their zeal and enthusiasm. With a wounded consciousness they cannot radiate hope. This becomes a vicious circle. Defeated/demotivated/demoralized teachers cannot become role models, and as a result, teaching as a vocation fails to attract the new generation.

These are real difficulties and obstacles. I have, however, always believed in human wonders and possibilities. I have seen that some of the finest moments of our existence emerge when we overcome obstacles, and realize our creativity. True, teaching as a vocation is not in very good shape. Yet, amidst us we continue to find some great teachers who motivate and inspire. Not solely that. We find young people—yes, young people—who defy the 'practical' logic of hard economics, choose to become teachers, and strive for the vocation which, they believe, has its beauty, dignity and charm. Herein lies hope. And with this hope begins the quest for a new world.

NOTES

1. Taken from an ad of Jaypee Group published in the New Delhi edition of the *The Indian Express* (7.11.06).
2. From Faiz's famous poem 'This Harvest of Hopes'; it is translated by V.G. Kiernan (2006: 215).
3. See the way Adam Curle—yet another brilliant educationist—has recognized the immense potential of teaching:

   What the teacher can and should do is to stimulate our intellectual curiosity, impart sound judgement, teach us to think logically, give us a measure of balanced confidence in ourselves, in short be... a facilitator of learning. Nor is this the whole story, for if learning in the most complete sense is to occur, it must be reciprocal, the teacher and the student must share and exchange their knowledge, teaching each other. They must, in fact, be open to each other, and the teacher must be sufficiently aware to accept gratefully what he has to learn from the student (1973: 64).

4. Take, for instance a shocking report: '*3 teachers took turns to rape student in UP School*' published in the New Delhi edition of *The Indian Express*, New Delhi (01.01.08):

   Five days ago, when her geography teacher asked her to see him at home, the 16-year old school girl happily agreed because she needed help ahead of an examination. But when she got there, she found him with two other teachers from her school. The trio allegedly took turns to rape her after threatening to fail her in the examination. This incident at Hadha in Unnao, which has sent shockwaves across the district after it came to light yesterday, involved three teachers of the Adharsh Inter College.

   Indeed, when such things happen, we realize how difficult it is to retain the dignity of the vocation of teaching, and its higher principles. This gap further intensifies our cynicism.

References

Apple, Michael. 1979. *Ideology and Curriculum*. London: Routlege and Kegan Paul.

Barnett, Ronald. 1994. *The Limits of Competence: Knowledge, Higher Education and Society*. Buckingham: The Society for Research into Higher Education and Open University Press.

Barney, Darin. 2004. *The Network Society*. Cambridge: Polity Press

Bellah, Robert. 1970. *Beyond Belief: Essays on Religion in a Post-Traditional World*. New York: Harper and Row.

Bennett, Oliver. 2001. *Cultural Pessimism: Narratives of Decline in the Postmodern World*. Edinburgh: Edinburgh University Press.

Beteille, Andre. 1988. 'The Pursuit of Equality and the Indian University' in Singh, Amrik and Sharma, G.D. (eds). *Higher Education in India: The Social Context*. Delhi: Konark Publishers.

Bhatt, B.D. and Aggarwal, J.C. 1969. (eds). *Educational Documents in India (1831-1968)*. New Dellhi: Arya Book Depot.

Blackledge, David and Hunt, Barry. 1985. *Sociological Interpretations of Education*. New York: Routledge.

Bloch, Marc. 1954. *The Historian's Craft*. Manchester: Manchester University Press.

Bloom, Harold and Trilling, Lionel (eds). 1973. *Romantic Poetry and Prose*. New York: Oxford University Press.

Bok, Derek. 2003. *Universities in the Marketplace: The Commercialization of Higher Education*. Princeton and Oxford: Princeton University Press.

Brand, Keith. 1985. *Sun*. New Jersey: Troll Associates.

Braudel, Fernand. 1980. *On History*. Chicago: The University of Chicago Press.

Coombes, H. 1985. *Literature and Criticism*. Middlesex: Penguin Books.

Curle, Adam. 1973. *Education for Liberation*. London: Tavistock Publications Limited.

Devi Prasad. 1988. *Art: The Basis of Education*. New Delhi: National Book Trust.

Dewey, John. 1966. *Democracy and Education: An Introduction to the Philosophy of Education*. New York: The Free Press.

Dostoyevsky, F.D. 1983. *Stories*. Moscow: Raduga Publishers.

Dubey, S.C.1989. 'Professional Values' in Singh, Amrik and Sharma, G.D. (eds). *Higher Education in India: The Institutional Context*. Delhi: Konark Publishers.

Durkheim, Emile. 1933. *The Division of Labour in Society*. New York and London: The Free Press and Collier-Macmillan Limited.

———, 1956. *Education and Sociology*. New York, The Free Press.

———, 1961. *Moral Education: A Study in the Theory and Application of the Sociology of Education*. New York: The Free Press.

———, 1965. *The Elementary Forms of the Religious Life*. New York: The Free Press.

Feyerabend, P.K. 1975. *Against Method: Outline of an Anarchist Theory of Knowledge*. London: New Left Books.

———, 1987. *Science in a Free Society*. Manchester: Verso.

Foucault, Michel. 1982. *Discipline and Punish: The Birth of the Prison*. Middlesex: Penguin Books.

Freire, Paulo. 1972. *Pedagogy of the Oppressed*. Middlesex: Penguin Books.

Freud, Sigmund. 1985. *Civilization, Society and Religion, Group Psychology, Civilization and Its Discontents, and Other Works*. Middlesex: Penguin Books.

Fromm, Erich. 1979. *To Have or To Be*. London: Abacus.

———, 1980. *The Fear of Freedom*. London: Routledge and Kegan Paul.

———, 1985. *The Art of Loving*. London: Unwin Paperbacks.

Gabbard, David A. 2003. 'Education is Enforcement! The Centrality of Compulsory Schooling in Market Societies' in Saltman, Kenneth J and Daid A. (eds). *Education as Enforcement: The Militarization and Corporatization of Schools*. New York and London: Routledge Falmer.

Gandhi, M.K. 1953. *Towards New Education*. Ahmedabad: Navajivan Publishing House.

———, 1976. *An Autobiography or the Story of My Experiments with Truth*. Ahmedabad: Navajivan Press.

———, 1982. *The Bhagvadgita*. Delhi: Orient Paperbacks.

Giddens, Anthony. 1993. *New Rules of Sociological Method: A Positive Critique of Interpretative Sociologies*. Stanford: Stanford University Press.

Giroux, Henry. 1997. 'Crossing the Boundaries of Educational Discourse: Modernism, Postmodernism and Feminism' in Hasley, A.H.; Lauder, Hugh; Brown, Philip; and Wells, Amy Stuart (eds).

Education: Culture, Economy and Society. Oxford and New York: Oxford University Press.

Griffith, Ralph T.H. 1971. *The Hymns of the RigVeda, Vol. I, II*. Varanasi: The Chowkhama Sanskrit Series Office.

Government of India. 1966. *Report of the Education Commission, 1964-66*. New Delhi: Ministry of Education, Govt. of India.

———, 2007. *National Knowledge Commission: Report to the Nation*, 2006.

Gramsci, Antonio. 1971. *Selections from the Prison Notebooks*. London: Lawrence and Wishart.

Guha, Ranjit (ed) 1994. *Subaltern Studies I: Writings on South Asian History and Society*. Delhi: Oxford University Press.

Habermas, Jurgen. 2004. *Knowledge and Human Interests*. Cambridge: Polity Press.

Hayward, Tim. 1994. *Ecological Thought: An Introduction*. Cambridge: Polity Press.

Hobsbawm, Eric. 1996. *The Age of Extremes: A History of the World, 1914-1991*. New York: Vintage Books.

Hollingdale, R.J. (ed). 1981. *A Nietzsche Reader*. Middlesex: Penguin Books.

Jung, C.G. 1967. *The Spirit in Man, Art and Literature*. London, Melbourne and Henley: Ark Books.

Kaul, Kadambari. 2007. *Voices from the Dhammapada*. New Delhi: Indialog Publications.

Kerr, Clark. 1963. *The Uses of the University*. New York: Harper and Row.

Kiernan,V.C.G. 2006. *Poems by Faiz*. Delhi: Oxford University Press.

Kuhn, Thomas S. 1970. *The Structure of Scientific Revolutions*. London: University of Chicago Press.

Kumar, Arun. 1989. 'Teachers Today' in Singh, Amrik and Sharma, G.D. (eds). *Higher Education in India: The Institutional Context*. Delhi: Konark Publishers.

Kumar, Krishna. 1996. *Learning from Conflict*. New Delhi: Orient Longman.

Lyons, F.S.L. 1983. 'The Idea of a University: Newman to Robbins' in Phillipson, Nicholas (ed). *Universities, Society and the Future*. Edinburgh: Edinburgh University Press.

Mannheim, Karl and Stewart. W.A.C. 1962. *An Introduction to the Sociology of Education*. London: Routledge and Kegan Paul.

Marx, Karl. 1977. *Economic and Philosophic Manuscripts of 1844*. Moscow: Progress Publishers.

Merton, Robert. 1972. *Social Theory and Social Structure*. Delhi: Macmillan.

Nehru, Jawaharlal. 1983. *The Discovery of India*. New Delhi: Jawaharlal Nehru Memorial Fund.

———, 1984. *An Autobiography*. New Delhi: Jawaharlal Nehru Memorial Fund.

———, 1989. *Glimpses of World History*. New Delhi: Jawaharlal Nehru Memorial Fund.

Newman, J.H.1959. *The Idea of a University*. New York: Image Books.

Niblett, Roy. 1994. 'Levels of Discord' in Barnett, Ronald (ed). *Academic Community: Discourse or Discord*. London and Bristol: Jessica Kingsley Publishers.

Oommen, T.K. 1997. *Citizenship, Nationality and Ethnicity: Reconciling Competing Identities*. Cambridge: Polity Press.

Parsons, Talcott. 1968. 'The School Class as a Social System: Some of its Functions in American Society' in Bell, Robert and Stab, Holger R. (eds). The *Sociology of Education: A Source book*. Homewood: The Dorsey Press.

Passmore, John. 1978. *Science and Its Critics*. London: Duckworth.

Pathak, Avijit. 1998. *Indian Modernity: Contradictions, Paradoxes and Possibilities*. Delhi: Gyan Publishing House.

———, 2002. *Social Implications of Schooling: Knowledge, Pedagogy and Consciousness*. Delhi: Rainbow.

———, 2006. *Modernity, Globalization and Identity: Towards a Reflexive Quest*. Delhi: Aakar Books.

Pattison, M. 1876. 'Address on Education' in *Transactions of the National Association for the Promotion of Social Sciences*. London.

Playfair, L. 1889. *Subjects of Social Welfare*. London.

Popper, K.R. 1972. *Conjectures and Refutations*. London: Routledge and Kegan Paul.

Postman, Neil and Weingartner, Charles. 1971. *Teaching as a Subversive Activity*. Middlesex: Penguin Books.

Pusey, Michael. 1987. *Jurgen Habermas*. Chichester & London: Ellis Horwood Ltd/Tavistok Publications.

Radhakrishnan, S. 1953. *The Principal Upanishads*. London: George Allen and Unwin Ltd.

———, 1976. *The Bhagavadgita*. Bombay: Blackie and Son Ltd.

Rose, Hilary. 1994. *Love, Power and Knowledge: Towards a Feminist Transformation of the Sciences*. Cambridge: Polity Press.

Sarkar, Sumit. 1983. *Modern India: 1885-1997*. Delhi: Macmillan India Limited.

Scott-James, R.A. 1956. *The Making of Literature*. London: Secker and Warburg.

Shils, Edward. 1977. 'Social Sciences as Public Opinion' in *Minerva*, Vol. 15, Nos. 3-4.

———, 1982. 'The Academic Ethic' in *Minerva,* Vol. 20, Nos. 1-2.

———, 1992. 'The Service of Society and the Advancement of Learning in the Twenty-First Century' in *Minerva* Vol. 30, No. 2.

Shukla, P.D. 1988. *The New Education Policy in India*. New Delhi: Sterling Publishers.

Singh, Amrik. 1989. 'Managing Students' in Singh, Amrik and Sharma, G.D. (eds). *Higher Education in India: The Institutional Context:* Delhi: Konark Publishers.

Singha, H.S. 1984. *Public Examinations: A Critique*. New Delhi: Vikas Publishing House.

Snow, C.P. 1964. *The Two Cultures and a Second Look*. New York: Mentar.

Spring, Joel H. 1972. *Education and the Rise of the Corporate State*. Boston: Becan Press.

Sri Aurobindo. 1977. *The Human Cycle*. Pondicherry: Sri Aurobindo Ashram.

Tagore, Rabindranath. 1983a. 'The Religion of an Artist' in *Vision of India*. New Delhi: Indian Council for Cultural Relations.

———, 1983b. 'A Poet's School' in *Vision of India*. New Delhi: Indian Council for Cultural Relations.

Uberoi, J.P.S. 2002. *The European Modernity: Science, Truth and Method*. New Delhi: Oxford University Press.

Usher and Edwards. 1994. *Postmodernism and Education*. London and New York: Routledge.

Weber, Max. 1948. 'Science as a Vocation' in Gerth and Mills (eds). *From Max Weber: Essays in Sociology*. London: Routledge and Kegan Paul.

Whitman, Walt. 1986. *Leaves of Grass*. New Delhi: Prentice-Hall of India.

Index